MADDIE MOATE

ILLUSTRATED BY PAUL BOSTON

PUFFIN

CONTENTS

Hello there, or should I say,

MERRY CHRISTMAS!

OK, so it might not be Christmas Day as you're reading this, but the chances are we're probably getting close. Perhaps it's a month away? A few weeks? Days? HOURS?!

If Christmas Day is only a few hours away, that means it's Christmas Eve. So you should put this book down and go straight to sleep because a special someone might be paying you a visit any moment now! You know who I'm talking about.

FATHER CHRISTMAS!

Excuse me. That was Puddles and Nigel. I'll introduce them in a bit.

I'm Maddie, by the way. You might know me from my YouTube adventures about science and wildlife. Or maybe you've watched my television programmes about how things work? If you have, then you already know that I *love* to ask questions. But do you know what else I love? Christmas!

Christmas is one of my favourite times of the year, so I thought it would be fun to find out as much about it as I possibly could. I want to know *why* we celebrate Christmas and do some of the curious things we do, such as hang stockings, eat Brussels sprouts and pull crackers that go *BANG*! And I'm also interested in how people all around the world celebrate Christmas, and all the other fascinating festivals that happen in wintertime.

I won't be going on this curious Christmas quest alone, though. Let me introduce you to Puddles and Nigel, my (not so helpful) Christmas helpers.

HEY!

Puddles is an Adélie penguin from Antarctica. She's only little, but she's bursting with energy, brilliant at sports, and *loves* to learn – especially when the subject is Christmas . . . or sardines.

HELLO!

And this is Nigel, an abominable snowman – also known as a yeti. He used to live in the Himalayan mountains in Nepal, but he moved to the Arctic just to be closer to Father Christmas (Nigel is Father Christmas's BIGGEST fan!). Nigel sometimes forgets how big he is and can be a bit clumsy, so please bear with him.

I've also sprinkled some magical Christmas activities and experiments throughout the book for you to try at home – and this is where you'll meet Big Elf.

HI!

Big Elf is a hard-working and trustworthy senior elf (you might have one in your home – they also go by the name 'Grown-Up'). They'll be on hand to help us with all the fun activities – especially the messy ones!

So, that's our merry gang. Are you ready to join us on a curious Christmas fact-finding mission?

5

I thought you might be.

(Before we start, there's something else to look out for –
we've hidden twenty-five gingerbread men like this one
for you to find throughout the book. See if you can
spot them all before Nigel and Puddles gobble
them up!)

On your marks, get set . . . HO HO HO!

TRADITIONS AND CULTURES

Let's kick things off with some of the big, important questions. What is Christmas anyway? And where do our Christmas traditions come from? Although Christmas is celebrated worldwide, the traditions we look forward to can vary depending on where we live and what we believe.

So, let's explore some familiar favourites and slightly more curious traditions, from stockings stuffed with presents to sausage-snatching Icelandic trolls!

WHAT IS CHRISTMAS?

What does Christmas mean to you? For me, Christmas is a time to spend with my family.

- It's a time to play games, watch movies, listen to music and tell stories.
- It's a time to decorate the house and bring a bit of sparkle to the long, cold days.
- It's a time to give gifts and send messages to my loved ones.

That's a pretty good summary of MY kind of Christmas, but YOURS might look very different. As the year comes to a close, millions of people worldwide will look forward to enjoying Christmas in their own special ways, too.

There is no ONE way to celebrate Christmas. However, most people (whether they are religious or not) recognize Christmas as a Christian festival that celebrates the birth of Jesus. We can break the word down to help us understand what it means.

Christ = Jesus Christ
Mass = The name of a service where Christians remember the life of Jesus and think about all the kind things he did.
Christmas = A special celebration when Christians celebrate the birth of Jesus Christ.

Many Christians will celebrate the birth of Jesus by going to church. For some, it's a yearly tradition to tell the story of Jesus's birth. We call this the Nativity Story. Perhaps you've been in a Nativity play at school? I once got to play the part of an angel, and my mum made me a white tunic out of a bed sheet and a halo out of a coat hanger.

I THOUGHT I LOOKED EXTREMELY COOL.

In case you've forgotten what the Nativity Story is all about, here's a quick reminder of the main characters:

Mary
A young woman set to marry Joseph. She's pretty surprised when an angel shows up in her bedroom and announces she will have God's baby.

Angel Gabriel
The angel who delivers God's message to Mary. (Also called an archangel, which is basically like the boss of all angels.)

Joseph
A carpenter engaged to Mary. Seems pretty chilled about the whole 'message from God' thing.

The donkey
The unsung hero of the story – carries Mary all the way to Bethlehem, where she is going to give birth.

The innkeeper
An all-round nice guy who lets Mary and Joseph stay in his stable when there's no room in any inns.

Baby Jesus
The star of the show! He is born in a manger (a sort of feeding bucket for animals).

The Three Kings
Fancy royal gentlemen who follow a star to find the baby Jesus and bring him gifts.

The shepherds
This lot are also surprised by an angel who leads them (and their sheep) to where Jesus is born in the stable.

What do Spanish sheep say at Christmas time?
Fleece Navidad!

You may have heard a slightly different version of the Nativity. Nowadays, it's pretty common for schools to add their own twist and turn it into an all-singing, all-dancing show. I know of one version that included a gang of cowboys, and another with some comedy hairdressers. However, my absolute favourite featured some funky camels and a disco-dancing star who takes part in a dazzling dance show titled Lights, Camel, Action! It's Strictly the Nativity.

THE POOPING MAN!

In Catalonia, Spain, the Nativity scene has an extra character hidden among the traditional figures. If you look closely, beyond Mary, Joseph and the usual suspects, you'll spot a man crouching down to do a poo! This man is called the *caganer*, which means 'defecator', and he regularly makes a Christmas appearance in Catalonia. It might seem rude to have a pooping man in the Nativity scene, but Catalonians don't see it like this. For them, the *caganer* is good fun and a tradition that has been around for years. It's also true that throughout history, pooping has been linked to health and good luck, so why not have this symbol in the Christmas story?

Sorry, I was distracted by a pooping man. Where were we? Oh yes. What is Christmas?

Christmas can be celebrated in many ways, but it has roots as a Christian festival that honours the birth of Jesus. However, not everyone who celebrates Christmas is religious. For many people, it is simply a holiday when family and friends can enjoy spending time together. There's also the added bonus that some people – especially children – are lucky enough to get presents. Did I hear someone say,

FATHER CHRISTMAS!

Don't you worry, I'll get to him very soon.

WHY IS CHRISTMAS ON 25 DECEMBER?

The simple answer to this question is:

WE DON'T KNOW!

JUST KIDDING! That answer wouldn't be very satisfying, would it? Let's start again.

WHY IS CHRISTMAS ON 25 DECEMBER?

I had always thought 25 December was Jesus's birthday. However, nobody actually knows when it is! The Bible doesn't mention any date of birth, so who decided we should celebrate Christmas on the twenty-fifth?

There are a few different ideas as to why 25 December was picked for the big day. It's almost impossible to prove any of them *more* right than the other, but they're all fascinating stories, and the unknown is always worth investigating.

WHOSE BIRTHDAY IS IT?

One early Christian story suggests that Mary (Jesus's mother) was told on 25 March that she was going to have a special baby. It takes nine months for a baby to grow, and nine months after 25 March is . . . 25 December! This is a pretty convincing theory, but it's likely there's a lot more to it.

The first 'official' recording of Christmas being celebrated on 25 December was during the time of the first Christian Roman emperor, Constantine, in 336 CE (that's more than 1,685 years ago!). However, in 336 CE there were lots of other cultural festivals happening in and around December, so perhaps it made sense for Christians to honour Jesus's birthday at a similar time.

WINTER SOLSTICE

One of these festivals was the **winter solstice**. This is when there is the shortest amount of time between the Sun rising and the Sun setting, making it the longest night and shortest day of the year. The Romans celebrated winter solstice as a time to say goodbye to the long, dark days and welcome the return of the Sun. It usually happened on 21 or 22 December, but it can fall on 20 or 23 December. Pretty close to 25 December, don't you think? Maybe the winter solstice was the inspiration for celebrating Christmas around this time. (You can learn more about the science of the winter solstice on page 90!)

SATURNALIA

Another Roman festival closely linked to the winter solstice was **Saturnalia**. It started out as a farmers' festival because it was a time to celebrate Saturn, the god of planting seeds, but it soon became a big party for everybody. Servants and their masters would even eat and drink together, which NEVER happened at any other time of the year. The Roman poet Statius described crowds of partygoers being showered with sweets, nuts and fruit – and even flamingos being released to fly over Rome!

?
DID YOU KNOW . . .
that the name for a group of flamingos is a flamboyance? How fancy!

Some people think that our Christmas traditions of eating, drinking and giving and receiving presents may have roots in the celebrations of Saturnalia (although the festive flamingos clearly didn't catch on). Originally, Saturnalia was held on 17 December, but it later became a seven-day holiday and stretched all the way to 23 December.

HANUKKAH

The Jewish Festival of Lights, **Hanukkah**, also takes place in December, though the dates change every year depending on the Hebrew calendar. The Hanukkah story goes back over 2,000 years to when the Jewish people won a battle for religious freedom. They lit an oil lamp to honour their victory, and although the lamp only had enough oil to stay lit for one night, it miraculously burned for eight days! (You can find out more about modern-day Hanukkah celebrations on pages 54–59.)

Hanukkah is its own Jewish festival and shouldn't be confused with Christmas. However, Jesus himself was Jewish, so it's possible that Hanukkah may have had something to do with why we now celebrate Jesus's birth during the month of December.

Those are just some of the theories about why 25 December came to be Christmas Day. But did you know that some people have their celebrations on a completely different day altogether?

LET'S FIND OUT WHY . . .

WHAT ARE THE TWELVE DAYS OF CHRISTMAS?

'On the first day of Christmas,
my true love gave to me . . .
a partridge in a pear tree!'

Do you know this song? The 'Twelve Days of Christmas' is a well-known Christmas carol that we hear throughout December. It's played EVERYWHERE: in shops, on the radio, on the telly. You might even sing it at school!

The song works like a memory game – the whole point is to try to remember the previous verses while adding a new one each time. It's about one lucky person who receives a lot of Christmas presents from their true love. And when I say a lot, I mean a LOT.

I wonder if you can work out how many presents the person gets in total? Do you think you could try to add them all up? Grab a pencil and some scrap paper and see how you do. I'll help start you off.

'On the first day of Christmas,
my true love sent to me
A partridge in a pear tree.'

On this day, the person gets one present.
(One partridge in a pear tree)
1

'On the second day of Christmas,
my true love sent to me
Two turtle doves,
And a partridge in a pear tree.'

On this day the person gets three presents.
(Two turtle doves + one partridge in a pear tree)
2+1=3

'On the third day of Christmas,
my true love sent to me
Three french hens
Two turtle doves,
And a partridge in a pear tree.'

On this day, the person gets six presents.
(Three French hens + two turtle doves + one partridge in a pear tree)
3+2+1=6

The song carries on, adding . . .

Four calling birds
Five golden rings
Six geese a-laying
Seven swans a-swimming
Eight maids a-milking
Nine ladies dancing
Ten lords a-leaping
Eleven pipers piping
Twelve drummers drumming

TURN THE PAGE FOR
THE ANSWER!

If you add up all the gifts from all twelve days, the person receives a whopping . . .

364 PRESENTS!

How did you do?!

The mystery gift-giver is extremely generous, but to be honest I'm not sure what anyone would do with all those presents. I mean, 184 of them are birds. Just think of all the bird poo! And where would you put 140 people drumming, piping and leaping all over the place? No thanks; that sounds far too noisy. What's wrong with some chocolate coins or a train set?

Knock, knock.
Who's there?
Anna.
Anna who?
Anna Partridge in a Pear Tree.

Thankfully, it's very unlikely that anyone will be receiving all those presents, because it's just a bit of made-up fun. However, the Twelve Days of Christmas definitely ARE a real thing. Although they aren't the twelve days in the run-up to Christmas like you might expect – they're actually the twelve days *after*.

EPIPHANY

The Twelve Days of Christmas are the twelve days from 25 December (Christmas Day) all the way up to 6 January. This is thought to be the amount of time it took the Three Kings (also known as the Wise Men or Magi) to follow a star to Bethlehem, where they discovered the newborn Baby Jesus.

6 January is sometimes called 'Epiphany', and the evening of 5 January is 'Epiphany Eve'. The word 'Epiphany' comes from the Greek word meaning 'to appear', and this is when Baby Jesus appeared before the Three Kings. In some parts of the world, Epiphany and the arrival of the Three Kings is just as important as Christmas Day.

- **In Spain and parts of Latin America, Epiphany, or 'Three Kings Day', is a big celebration when people exchange their Christmas gifts. Some cities have parades with music, decorated floats and even REAL camels!**
- **In the Czech Republic, brave swimmers take an icy plunge and celebrate Epiphany by jumping into the freezing cold Vltava river.**
- **In Belgium, children dress up as the Three Kings and go from door to door to sing songs in return for money and sweets. (It's a bit like trick or treating at Halloween!)**

But there's one thing a lot of countries' Epiphany celebrations have in common: cake!

Rosca de Reyes, or 'round bread of kings', is a special ring-shaped bread that is eaten in Mexico. Before the bread is sliced open, a tiny plastic baby is hidden inside. The baby represents Jesus, and whoever finds it is supposed to get good luck! The Spanish version of Rosca de Reyes hides an extra surprise: a dry bean buried in the dough. If you find the bean, you'll have all the luck – BUT you also have to buy the cake next Christmas!

Galette des Rois, or 'cake of kings', is a type of flat almond tart that the French enjoy on Epiphany. It's usually decorated with a gold paper crown and baked with a little charm – known as a *fève* – tucked away inside. If you find the *fève*, you have to wear the paper crown AND you also get announced as king or queen for the day. Fancy!

So, for some people, the Twelve Days of Christmas is a fun Christmas carol featuring 364 ridiculous presents. But for others, it's an exciting time in the run-up to Epiphany and their biggest day of festive celebrations and gift-giving.

SURELY it's time to talk about Father Christmas now?!

OK, I did promise – let's find out all about this mystery man!

WHO IS FATHER CHRISTMAS?

Father Christmas goes by many names. You may know him as **Santa**, **Santa Claus**, **Père Noël**, **Baba Noël**, **Kris Kringle** or even **St. Nick**. For the purposes of this book, we're going to stick with Father Christmas. But who is he?

It's almost impossible to know anything for certain about Father Christmas because he's a legend – a character known throughout history, with a magical and mysterious lifestyle. All around the world, people have a different idea of who Father Christmas is – here are just a few examples:

UK AND THE USA – FATHER CHRISTMAS/SANTA CLAUS

The Father Christmas that I know is a jolly old gentleman with a white beard, who wears a red suit and a chunky black belt. He lives in the North Pole in a magical toy workshop run by elves, and on Christmas Eve he delivers presents to children using a sleigh pulled by flying reindeer.

How do we know that father Christmas is good at karate? Because he has a black belt!

25

GHANA – PAPA BRONYA

In Ghana, Father Christmas is known as Papa Bronya and wears a beautiful red-and-gold robe and sandals, a traditional patterned sash and a white hood. Instead of leaving behind toys, Papa Bronya likes to leave treats for children to eat.

RUSSIA, SLOVENIA, UKRAINE – DED MOROZ AND SNEGUROCHKA

Ded Moroz means 'Grandfather Frost' and is thought to be an ancient snow wizard who carries a magical staff. He wears long, luxurious robes in blue or red, a furry cap, felt boots and rides on a sleigh pulled by three white horses. Ded Moroz is often joined by his granddaughter, Snegurochka, which means 'snowmaiden'.

HAWAII – KANAKALOKA

Aloha! In Hawaii, Father Christmas goes by the name 'Kanakaloka'. This cool dude is often seen sporting a tropical Hawaiian shirt and red swimming trunks. He comes to Hawaii not on a sleigh, but cruising in a red outrigger canoe. How totally awesome.

JOULUPUKKI – FINLAND

In Finland, Father Christmas is known as 'Joulupukki', which means 'Christmas Goat'. These days, Joulupukki looks very similar to Father Christmas, but Finnish people used to imagine him as a scary half-man, half-goat who would steal presents! The name stuck, but thankfully the days of the mean old Christmas goat are long gone.

OK, so we know not all versions of Father Christmas look, or act, the same – but a lot of them look like an old man with a beard wearing a red suit. Why is that?

WHY DOES FATHER CHRISTMAS WEAR RED?

Father Christmas is incredibly good at what he does. His literal job description is to deliver gifts WITHOUT BEING SEEN – he's an international man of mystery! So, if nobody has actually seen him, how do we know what he looks like?

Over the years, Father Christmas has been pictured in all sorts of colours. He's been painted in brown and green for a natural, 'man of the forest' kind of look, and purple and gold for a touch of glam. But he always seems to come back to red.

There's no doubt Father Christmas looks fabulous in red. It's what we see him wearing in movies, in adverts and on the front of Christmas cards. But why not blue? Or pink? Or rainbow stripes?

Before we take a whistle-stop tour of the history of Father Christmas and his clothes, I should probably say that the image we have of him today is a magnificent mishmash of ideas from all around the world and the work of countless artists. These are just some of the highlights!

Where to begin?

**IT'S COKE!
COCA-COLA!
IT'S DEFINITELY
COCA-COLA!**

LOTS of people believe that it was Coca-Cola who made Father Christmas red and white in order to match the colours of their famous logo. Although this is a tempting story, it isn't exactly true.

In 1931, Coca-Cola asked an illustrator called Haddon Sundblom to paint Father Christmas for some adverts. Those paintings featured Father Christmas wearing a red suit with a white beard, a smiley face, rosy cheeks, twinkling eyes and a tubby belly.

But – like you and I – Haddon Sundblom had never SEEN Father Christmas, nor was his picture a completely original idea. Instead, Sundblom took inspiration from a poem known as 'The Night Before Christmas'. Have you heard of it? It was written by a New Yorker called Clement Clarke Moore in 1882. Here are some of the best bits of him describing Father Christmas:

His eyes – how they twinkled! his dimples, how merry!
His cheeks were like roses, his nose like a cherry!

He had a broad face and a little round belly
That shook when he laughed, like a bowl full of jelly.

So was it the poet Clement Clarke Moore who designed Father Christmas as we know him?

Ummm, not really.

Moore's hometown of New York was founded by Dutch people, and in the 1800s, the Dutch version of Father Christmas would have been familiar to the people who lived there. 'Sinterklaas' was the Dutch name for Father Christmas, and they imagined him to look like a kind old man wearing . . . RED ROBES! Sound familiar?

So Moore's description of Father Christmas was probably inspired by Sinterklaas! Not exactly original. However, Moore WAS the first person to describe him as – ahem – a bit chubby.

(Of course, we don't know – nor should we comment – on the state of Father Christmas's true figure . . . but if you ask me, I reckon he's HENCH and covered in muscles! Surely that would make sense for a man who carries tons of presents and wrangles reindeer?)

So was it the Dutch who decided Father Christmas should wear red?

STILL NO.

The Dutch idea of Sinterklaas has roots in something EVEN older! Sinterklaas was inspired by Saint Nicholas, a fourth-century Greek bishop from Myra (now in modern-day Turkey), who was said to have given gifts to the poor – especially children. And bishops at the time wore red robes. **BINGO!**

Very little is known of the historical Saint Nicholas's life, although he's thought to have been born in Roman times, around 270 CE – a VERY long time ago. So it turns out we can trace our modern idea of Father Christmas all the way back over a thousand years to this kindly old bishop.

Where does Santa store his suit?
In his Claus-et.

WHY DO WE GET PRESENTS IN STOCKINGS?

One of my favourite festive traditions is leaving out a stocking for Father Christmas to fill with presents. Do you have a stocking too? Maybe your stocking looks like a sock for giants, or perhaps you use a pillowcase? Hanging stockings by the fireplace is a tradition that children in parts of Europe and the USA have been enjoying for a very long time. But where did the tradition come from?

Do you remember Saint Nicholas, the fourth-century Greek bishop from Myra? (That really is a very long name – let's just call him St. Nick from now on.) Throughout history, people around the world have told hundreds of stories about St. Nick's kindness and generosity. In fact, he was so popular that he became the patron saint of LOADS of things.

(A patron saint is supposed to help people with a particular need, like a good harvest, for example.)

Among the long list of things that St. Nick is meant to be the saint of are sailors, merchants, archers, children, beer makers and wolves. Apparently, he's the patron saint of wolves because he once helped a bunch of shepherds protect their sheep from a hungry wolf. What a great guy!

But while we don't often talk about St. Nick saving sheep any more, there's one story about him that has stuck around. It goes something like this . . .

Once upon a time, a father of three girls was having some money trouble. His daughters were beautiful, but he worried that being poor would make it impossible for them to marry.

(This story comes from the olden times when people thought that girls HAD to get married to a man to be successful. And in order to get married, you HAD to have money to offer the man's family. Of course, nowadays we know that girls can be perfectly happy and successful without getting married.)

St. Nick heard about the family's problems and wanted to help them, but he knew the father would be too proud to accept charity. So, one night, St. Nick crept up to the house and threw three bags of gold coins through the window (most houses didn't have chimneys back then!). The coins fell into the girls' stockings, which were drying by the fire.

The girls woke up in the morning and were DELIGHTED to discover their new treasure. Because of St. Nick's kindness, the three daughters were now rich enough to marry, and their father no longer had to worry about how they would be taken care of. It's this story that is said to have inspired the tradition of putting out stockings for Father Christmas to fill with gifts.

How does Father Christmas feel when he gets stuck in a chimney?

Claus-trophobic!

Another thing you may have wondered is, why do we get oranges in stockings? It turns out that in some versions of the story, St. Nick left three solid-gold balls instead of bags of coins. Solid-gold balls aren't very easy to get hold of (even for Father Christmas), so over the years, they have been replaced with something delicious that looks similar – an orange! Satsumas and clementines are often used in stockings today as they're easy to peel and eat.

I love eating satsumas – but here's how you can have some fun with a cool satsuma science experiment before you gobble them up!

SINKING SATSUMAS

Unlike St. Nick, we won't be dropping satsumas into anybody's socks (nobody wants oranges squashed between their toes!), but we are going to drop one into a jug of water for this experiment.

You will need
- a satsuma (any kind of orange will work!)
- a clear jug of water (you can use any clear container as long as it's big enough for the satsuma to fit and tall enough for it to move up and down.)

Instructions

Make sure you ask permission from your Big Elf (a grown-up) before you experiment with water.

1 Prepare your jug and think about what might happen when you drop your satsuma into the water. Will it sink or will it float? Make your best guess and give it a go.

2 Now peel the satsuma. What do you think will happen when you put it in the water this time? Drop the peeled satsuma into the water to find out.

Did the experiment go as you expected? You might have thought the peel would make the orange heavier and sink. And perhaps you guessed that peeling the orange would make it lighter so it would float? However, the opposite happened! Why do you think that is?

THE SCIENCE BIT – WHAT MAKES THE SATSUMA SINK OR FLOAT?

The reason why an object sinks or floats is down to something called **density**. Everything in the world is made of tiny particles that we can't see called **atoms**. The density of a thing depends on how heavy its atoms are and how closely those atoms are packed together. If we could zoom in on a peeled orange, we'd see that its atoms are tightly squished together, so we can describe the fruit as **dense**. However, if we could zoom in on some orange peel, we'd see that its atoms are spread out with a bit more space between them. In this case, we would say that the peel is less dense than the flesh. Things will float on water if they have the same density, or are less dense, than the water they are in.

Density

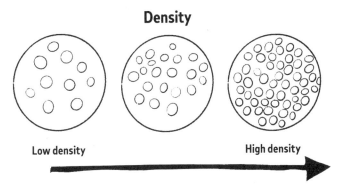

Low density

High density

The orange *with* the peel is less dense than water, so it floats! It's also full of tiny pockets of air, which give the orange something we call **buoyancy**. It's a bit like the orange is wearing a little life jacket that helps it get pushed to the surface! Peeling the orange removes that life jacket, and because the unpeeled orange is denser than water, it will sink.

Bonus Experiment Idea!
Why not ask a Big Elf to help you find some other Christmas objects to experiment with? How about a walnut with and without its shell? Or two Christmas decorations similar in size but made of different materials?

HOW DO CHRISTMAS PRESENTS GET DELIVERED?

Father Christmas is known for delivering presents in a magical, flying sleigh pulled by reindeer, but did you know there are lots of other legendary gift-givers who visit children around the world? Here are some of my favourites!

THE YULE LADS FROM ICELAND

In Iceland, children don't have just one festive visitor, but thirteen! They are the 'Yule Lads', or, in Icelandic, *Jólasveinar*.

The Yule Lads are cheeky trolls (although they look a lot like tall, gangly elves) who love to steal things and play tricks on people. They are a family of brothers who live in the mountains, but on the thirteen nights leading up to Christmas they come into town one by one to visit children while they sleep.

Every night, just before they head to bed, Icelandic children will place a shoe in their bedroom window. If they've been good that day, then one of the Yule Lads will fill their shoe with sweets and small gifts. However, if they've been naughty, the Yule Lad will leave them a rotten potato! I promise I'm not making this up.

The Yule Lads are a crazy bunch of characters and they each have their own tricks – including the 'Sausage Snatcher' and the 'Yoghurt Gobbler' (yep, you guessed it – they like to pinch sausages and yoghurt!). But don't worry, Icelandic children know how to handle these mischief-makers. On the night the Yoghurt Gobbler is due to arrive, children might leave a yoghurt pot in their shoe to keep him happy (and make sure they don't wake up to a rotten potato!).

THE THREE KINGS

Children in Spanish-speaking countries also receive presents in their shoes, but instead of trolls, their gifts are delivered by royalty! You might remember from page 23 that Spain and parts of Latin America celebrate Three Kings Day (also known as Epiphany), when the Three Kings arrived in Bethlehem with gifts for Baby Jesus. The night before the celebration, children polish their shoes and leave them on a windowsill, along with some snacks for the Kings and their camels. If the children have been good, the Three Kings will fill their shoes with treats as they pass by on their long journey.

BUT WHO WERE THE THREE KINGS?

Turn the page to find out!

Gaspar (also known as Caspar)

The King of India who brings the gift of frankincense.

Frankincense is a sticky goo known as a resin that oozes from a boswellia tree. When it dries, it hardens and can be burned or used as perfume.

Balthazar

The King of Arabia who brings the gift of myrrh.

Myrrh is another type of sticky resin that comes from a tree, but this one was used by ancient Egyptians to make dead bodies smell nice when they mummified them. Gross!

Melchior

The King of Persia who brings the gift of gold.

Gold is a shiny precious metal that comes from the ground and has been used to make jewellery for at least 6,600 years!

These days, children are less keen on the likes of frankincense and myrrh (no mummification perfume for me, thanks!), so instead they write letters to Gaspar, Balthazar and Melchior asking for the gifts they want – just like how other children might write to Father Christmas.

LA BEFANA

While lots of Italian children will open presents on Christmas Day, many are also visited on Epiphany by a kind gift-giving witch called La Befana. (How lucky to get TWO rounds of presents!) La Befana is often described as an old woman, with a long nose and a pointy chin, a raggedy skirt and a shawl covered in patches. Oh, and she flies between houses on a broomstick with a sack full of sweets on her shoulder.

There are a few different stories about La Befana and why she delivers gifts, but one of the most common tales connects her to the Three Kings:

Legend has it that the Three Kings visited La Befana's house on their way to Bethlehem, and she took them in and made them feel welcome. In return, the Three Kings invited her to join them on their journey. But by the time she had cleaned the whole house and gathered a basket of gifts for Baby Jesus, the Kings had already left. La Befana searched and searched, but she couldn't catch up with them, so she decided to give the gifts to other children she met along the way.

These days, La Befana visits on Epiphany Eve (5 January) and leaves children a stocking full of sweets for being good and a lump of coal for the times they've been naughty. She's such a nice witch, even her coal is made of sugar – yum!

Italy isn't the only country that is visited by a festive witch. In Norway, some people hide their broomsticks on Christmas Eve as naughty witches and other spirits are said to come out, steal them and take them for a ride!

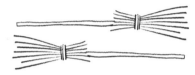

THE SMALLEST CAMEL IN SYRIA

Not everybody in Syria celebrates Christmas, but some people believe their Christmas gifts are delivered by a brave little camel.

The Three Kings are said to have rode camels on their long trek to Bethlehem. The story goes that the youngest and smallest of these camels was completely exhausted by the long journey, but he refused to give up because he was so determined to meet Baby Jesus. When the travelling group finally arrived at the stable, Jesus blessed the smallest camel with everlasting life in return for being so faithful throughout his difficult journey.

DID YOU KNOW . . .
A group of camels carrying people or goods is called a 'caravan'.

Since then, on Epiphany Eve, Syrian children invite the smallest camel to visit their own homes by leaving their shoes stuffed with hay and some water on the doorstep. In return for the food and water, the grateful camel will fill the children's shoes with gifts.

The Syrian camel is a now-extinct species that was once the biggest camel in the world. It existed 100,000 years ago and was 4 metres tall, which is about the same height as an elephant!

It's worth saying that all of these legendary gift-givers are very specific about who and when they visit. So it doesn't matter how much hay or how many yoghurt pots you stuff into your shoes, it's unlikely you'll get any bonus rounds of presents. Nice try, though.

WHY DO WE HAVE CHRISTMAS TREES?

Decorating the Christmas tree is one of my favourite traditions (or should that be TREE-dition?). My mum used to try and make sure that EVERY decoration on our Christmas tree was edible. (Except for the fairy lights. Please do not eat fairy lights, that would be a terrible idea.) We would spend hours decorating biscuits, hanging candy canes and stringing cranberries into garlands until we were left with something spectacular that smelt fresh, woody and slightly sickly sweet all at the same time. *Mmmm*, delicious.

You might have a different tree-dition in your family and decorate your tree with baubles, tinsel or handmade ornaments (flip to pages 102–103 and 181–182 for some brilliant DIY decoration ideas!). There are so many ways to decorate a tree for Christmas, but where did the tradition of bringing an outside tree inside begin?

Christmas trees are usually conifers such as spruce, fir and pines. They each have slightly different needle-like leaves, but the important thing is that they are all 'evergreen', which means they stay green all year round!

If you shake hands (or branches) with a conifer, you'll be able to tell what type of tree it is depending on how the needles feel.

- **Fir trees have flat, needle-like leaves that you can't roll between your fingers.**
- **Spruce trees have stiff, pointy, sharp needles that feel a bit like shaking hands with a hairbrush.**
- **Pine trees have needles that grow in bunches of two, three or five that feel kind of soft and tickly when you shake them.**

(Shaking hands with a tree isn't exactly a scientific technique, but I find it works pretty well!)

Why are Christmas trees bad knitters?
They keep losing their needles!

Evergreen trees have had special meanings for a really long time. Remember winter solstice and the celebration of the Sun returning after the long, dark winter? Well, ancient people held celebrations to honour this changing of the seasons and would decorate their homes with evergreen branches as a symbol that spring was on its way.

And what about the Roman festival of Saturnalia? (You can flip to page 16 to read more about it but imagine a **MASSIVE** midwinter party in the streets!) This was another ancient festival when evergreen branches were used for decorations as a happy reminder that farms would soon be green and loaded with crops.

So the tradition of bringing trees indoors may have started in ancient times, but when did we start stringing lights and dangling pretty things on their branches? This tradition is thought to have started about 500 years ago in western Germany. Around this time, German Christians often performed a popular play on 24 December called

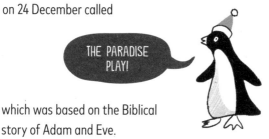

THE PARADISE PLAY!

which was based on the Biblical story of Adam and Eve.

(In case you haven't heard of Adam and Eve, they were a couple who lived in a beautiful place called the Garden of Eden, and in the centre of that garden was a tree loaded with fruit that they were not allowed to eat.)

One of the main props in this play was the 'paradise tree', which would be covered in the forbidden fruit. But because the play was performed in the winter, most fruit trees had lost all their leaves, so an evergreen tree decorated with apples was used instead. The tree was also hung with wafers and candles – both symbols of Jesus – in celebration of his birth. As the years passed, the wafers were replaced with pretty biscuits and other decorations such as paper flowers, nuts and sweets, which became part of what we now call the Christmas tree!

What did Adam say the day before Christmas?

It's Christmas, Eve.

Christmas trees didn't really become popular in England until Queen Victoria and her family made them fashionable. In 1848, a newspaper printed a picture of the royal family gathered around their beautiful Christmas tree – and soon everyone wanted their own magical tree fit for a queen!

These days, the most famous Christmas tree in England is probably the one that towers over London's Trafalgar Square. Since 1947, Norway has gifted the city of London a humongous spruce tree as a thank you for helping the Norwegian people during the Second World War.

The 30-metre-tall tree goes on an epic journey that starts just outside the capital of Norway, Oslo. Firstly, the tree is chopped down in Oslo's Nordmarka forest. Next, it is driven more than 66 miles to the port of Brevik, where it is loaded on to a ship and sets sail for the UK.

It then takes a lorry ride to Trafalgar Square, where a special team of people stands it up using a hydraulic crane! Last but not least, the tree is decorated in the Norwegian style with strings of lights going up and down the tree instead of around it. Now THAT is one big tree-dition!

I mentioned earlier that there are LOTS of ways to decorate a tree, and now we know that even the Norwegians have their own style of hanging lights, so let's find out about some more curious Christmas tree-ditions from around the world . . .

SPIDERWEBS IN UKRAINE

In Ukraine, it's common for people to decorate their Christmas trees with spiderwebs! This tradition comes from a sweet story about a mother and her two children. The family were very poor, so they couldn't afford ornaments to decorate their Christmas tree. But on Christmas Eve, a kind spider took pity on the family and covered their tree with spiderwebs. When the family woke on Christmas morning, the sun shone through the window and they were dazzled by the beautiful glistening webs. From that day on, the family decided they would always be grateful for what they had, and not worry about the things they didn't. Spiderwebs have since become a symbol of good luck, which is why Ukrainians hang them on their trees today.

UPSIDE-DOWN CHRISTMAS TREES

Some people choose to hang their Christmas trees upside down! This might seem an odd way to display a tree, but it's actually a great way to save space. A Christmas tree is wide at the bottom and narrow at the top, so if it's hanging upside down, you save a lot of floor space. (VERY important for playing with toys on Christmas Day, I think you'll agree.) In Poland during the 1800s, it was common to chop the tops off Christmas trees and hang them upside down above the dinner table. Although we don't know exactly where it comes from, so this tree-dition might have much older roots . . . (Sorry, couldn't resist a tree joke!)

POPCORN ON A STRING

In the USA, some people like to string popcorn into fluffy, cloud-like garlands and drape them around their Christmas trees. I love doing this on my own Christmas tree because it makes my house smell like a cinema! The idea may have been inspired by German people who moved to America and came with their own traditions of decorating trees with nuts, fruit and other treats.

But there's an even older tradition of decorating with popcorn that goes back to the ancient Aztec civilization, in what is now Mexico. Over 500 years ago, the Aztecs used popcorn to make headdresses and decorate their clothes for special dances and celebrations. The Aztec language even has a word for the sound of popcorn popping: 'totopoca'. (If you say it out loud it really does sound like popcorn popping in a pan!)

TOTOPOCA!

HIDE THE PICKLE!

A modern tree-dition is the wonderfully silly game of hiding a pickle in your Christmas tree! (Not an actual pickle, but rather a pickle ornament.) The idea is that whoever finds the pickle first gets an extra present. It's a popular game in Germany and the midwestern USA, but no one knows exactly where the tradition came from.

However, we do know that Germans have a history of making beautiful glass tree ornaments, which became popular in American department stores in the 1880s. Some of those ornaments were made in the shape of fruits and vegetables, so perhaps one year, a store ordered a few too many boxes of glass pickles and came up with a fun game to try to sell them all?!

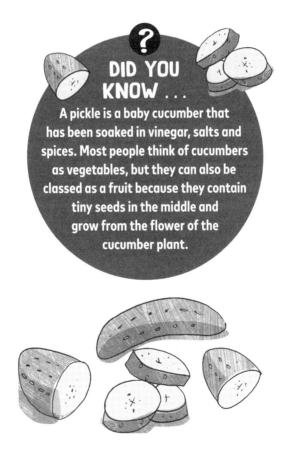

?

DID YOU KNOW . . .

A pickle is a baby cucumber that has been soaked in vinegar, salts and spices. Most people think of cucumbers as vegetables, but they can also be classed as a fruit because they contain tiny seeds in the middle and grow from the flower of the cucumber plant.

FOLDED MAGAZINE CHRISTMAS TREE

Whether you have a real tree, a plastic tree or an upside-down tree covered in spiderwebs and pickles, a Christmas tree is a beautiful way to fill your home with a bit of festive fun! I've got a thrifty Christmas craft idea for making your own tabletop Christmas tree using some very simple materials: a used magazine and a blob of glue.

You will need

- a used magazine
- PVA glue
- pencil
- scissors

Instructions

Make sure you ask a Big Elf to be on stand-by to help you with the scissors.

First, make sure anyone who wants to read the magazine has had a chance to! Then tear out one page (you will use this later). Fold the top right corner of the front cover to the middle of the magazine spine, creating a triangle shape.

Take the folded edge of the triangle and line it up with the magazine's spine to form another triangle.

Fold the overhanging point of the triangle upwards and tuck it inside the folds you have just made. This will give the tree a sturdy flat base.

Repeat the previous three steps until every magazine page is folded. The crisper and neater you can make your folds, the better. Once the folding is complete, stick the front and back covers together to transform them into a cone.

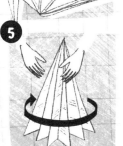

Arrange the folded triangles until you're happy with the look of your tree.

Great job! We're almost there. But for me, no Christmas tree is complete without something special on top!

6 Make a star by drawing and cutting out a star shape from the torn-out magazine page. Fold it down the middle to give it a 3D effect and use a blob of glue to stick it on.

Ta-da! Just like that, you have made a folded Christmas tree. If one star isn't enough for you, get creative and cut and stick as many paper decorations as you wish.

When you think about it, this crafty creation likely started out as an actual tree. That tree got chopped down and made into paper, which became a magazine, which has now been turned back into a tree! If you recycle your paper tree at the end of the holiday season, it might go on to be something else tree-based!

Wow, who knew there were so many different ways to decorate a Christmas tree?

Speaking of trees, there's another celebration that happens close to Christmas that also features a tree-like symbol. Can you guess what it is?

Erm, sorry Puddles, I'm not talking about your birthday (not sure how we arrived at that answer!). No, I'm talking about HANUKKAH! The tree-like symbol is called a **menorah**, and it's a type of lamp with several branches that has a special importance to the Jewish faith.

CURIOUS QUESTIONS ABOUT . . . HANUKKAH!

Here to tell us more about Hanukkah are two experts on the subject: Lazlo and Amber, who both celebrate Hanukkah at home with their families. Lazlo is eight years old and lives with his family in Brooklyn, USA, and Amber is five (nearly six) years old and lives with her family in London, England.

First up is Amber to tell us more about why Hanukkah is celebrated:

AMBER

LAZLO

THANKS FOR TALKING TO ME ABOUT HANUKKAH, AMBER! CAN YOU TELL ME WHAT IT IS AND HOW LONG IT LASTS FOR?

HANUKKAH USUALLY HAPPENS AROUND DECEMBER, AND IT ALWAYS LASTS FOR EIGHT DAYS.

WHY IS THAT?

IT'S BECAUSE OF THE HANUKKAH STORY! IT GOES LIKE THIS . . .

There once was a king called Antiochus who lived in Syria. And he didn't want the Jewish people to practise Judaism, so he captured their temple in Jerusalem and sent his army to attack them. But a small group of Jews called the Maccabees decided to fight back, and after lots of fighting, they won! But when the Jews got back to their temple, it was all messed up and almost everything was destroyed. They cleaned it up and wanted to light a lamp, but the only thing that hadn't been destroyed was a small bottle of oil – enough for one night. But then a miracle happened, because the small bottle of oil lasted EIGHT DAYS instead of one. The Jews recognized this was a miracle because it showed them that God is always with us.

WOW. WHAT A STORY. HOW DO YOU CELEBRATE THIS MIRACLE?

SO, YOU KNOW HOW THE OIL LASTED FOR EIGHT DAYS? WELL, WE LIGHT THE MENORAH FOR EIGHT DAYS.

I asked Lazlo to tell me a bit more about the menorah:

LAZLO, WHAT DOES A MENORAH LOOK LIKE AND HOW DOES IT WORK?

IT'S LIKE A BASE WITH NINE CANDLE HOLDERS: EIGHT CANDLES THAT YOU LIGHT EACH NIGHT AND ONE IN THE MIDDLE THAT YOU USE TO LIGHT ALL THE OTHERS. EVERY NIGHT OF HANUKKAH, YOU LIGHT ONE MORE CANDLE.

The special lamp that is lit on Hanukkah is commonly called a menorah, but the proper religious name for it is a *Chanukiah*, or a Hanukkah menorah. A menorah is actually an even more ancient type of lamp with *seven* candle holders – not nine – that was used in Jewish temples for centuries and is still used today as a symbol of Judaism around the world.

Of course, we couldn't talk about Hanukkah without discussing my *favourite* thing about holidays – food! Amber and Lazlo have two special food traditions they wanted to share with me. The first one is . . .

The oil used to fry *latkes* is thought to symbolize Hanukkah's miracle of oil. But interestingly, no one knows for sure when *latkes* first became a Hanukkah tradition. An earlier version of the *latke* was made with cheese instead of potato and is thought to have been inspired by a brave Jewish woman named Judith (or Yehudit). The story goes that Judith saved her village from an attacking army by feeding the army's general salty cheese and wine, causing him to fall asleep. Although this is not part of the Hanukkah story, Judith's victory is often remembered at Hanukkah. It's thought the cheesy pancakes were replaced with potato ones sometime in the nineteenth century, when Jewish people in eastern Europe relied on potatoes as an important source of food.

And the second food tradition is . . .

Gelt means money in Hebrew, which is the ancient language of the Jewish people. These foil-covered chocolate coins are often used as part of a game called *dreidel*. Lazlo explained to me how his family plays the game:

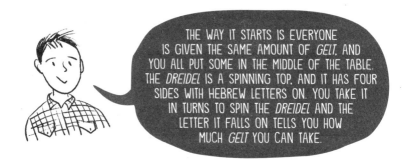

THE WAY IT STARTS IS EVERYONE IS GIVEN THE SAME AMOUNT OF *GELT*, AND YOU ALL PUT SOME IN THE MIDDLE OF THE TABLE. THE *DREIDEL* IS A SPINNING TOP, AND IT HAS FOUR SIDES WITH HEBREW LETTERS ON. YOU TAKE IT IN TURNS TO SPIN THE *DREIDEL* AND THE LETTER IT FALLS ON TELLS YOU HOW MUCH *GELT* YOU CAN TAKE.

Amber told me what all the Hebrew letters mean when the *dreidel* lands on them:

נ **Nun**, means nothing happens.

ש **Shin**, means you have to put a chocolate coin into the middle.

ה **Hey**, means you get half the chocolate coins.

ג **Gimel**, means you take all the chocolate coins!

This game sounds fun AND delicious! Finally, I asked Amber and Lazlo if there's anything else they love about Hanukkah.

PRESENTS!

YEAH! SOMETIMES KIDS GET EIGHT PRESENTS AND YOU GET TO OPEN ONE ON EACH DAY. AND WE ALSO GET TOGETHER WITH FRIENDS AND FAMILY FOR HANUKKAH PARTIES. THAT'S PROBABLY MY FAVOURITE THING OF ALL.

How awesome. I'm hoping I get invited for a game of *dreidel* soon!

MADDIE'S CURIOUS CHRISTMAS QUIZ – ROUND ONE

OK, I'm about to test whether you've been paying attention with my curious Christmas quiz! Let's see how much festive history you can remember . . .

1. What is the story of Jesus's birth called?
2. During the Roman festival of Saturnalia, what type of bird was said to fly over the crowds?
3. In the song, 'The Twelve Days of Christmas', how many presents does the person get given in total?
4. Which famous drinks company do people THINK made Father Christmas red?
5. What is the name of the poem that inspired a lot of people's thoughts about how Father Christmas looks?
6. Which bishop is thought to be the original inspiration for Father Christmas and the tradition of stockings?
7. How many Yule Lads are there in Iceland?
8. What are the three gifts famously given by the Three Kings?
9. Which country gifts the city of London the Trafalgar Square Christmas tree?
10. What unlikely 'fruit' do some people hide in their Christmas trees?

Answers on page 233

ANIMALS AND NATURE

When you think of a Christmas scene, what do you imagine? I bet it involves snow, some holly leaves – maybe even a prancing reindeer or two? For me, nature is a big part of what makes Christmas special (even though animals have literally no idea that Christmas is a thing).

Let's find out what makes winter wildlife so awesome, starting with . . .

HOW DO REINDEER FLY?

Sorry to disappoint you, but this type of magical know-how is reserved only for mythical creatures, supernatural folk and gift-giving legends.

My best guess is that in the lead-up to Christmas, the reindeer go through a magical change that alters their bone and hoof structure to make them extraordinarily lightweight and aerodynamic. I'd even go as far as to suggest they grow bat-like wings that they shed along with their antlers. But of course, this is only a theory and I have no solid evidence to back it up. Perhaps you could come up with your own theory for reindeer flight!

We may not know the secret to how they transform into magical flying beings, but we do know that reindeer are fascinating animals. I think reindeer should be appreciated all year round, not just at Christmas, so here are some other curious questions about their amazing (non-magical) features!

DO ALL REINDEER LIVE AT THE NORTH POLE?

Apart from the ones who live in Father Christmas's workshop, you're unlikely to find a reindeer at the North Pole. However, they do live very far north in the Arctic on vast open plains called the tundra. Tundra are some of the windiest and coldest places on Earth. But don't worry, reindeer have adapted to cope with all sorts of weather!

?

DID YOU KNOW . . .

that reindeer aren't always called reindeer? In North America, Canada, Alaska and Greenland, they are called caribou, while in northern Europe and Asia they're called reindeer.

DO REINDEER EAT CARROTS?

Do you leave anything for Rudolf and the reindeer to eat on Christmas Eve? I like to leave a couple of carrots outside for the gang to snack on, as carrots can't grow on the tundra so they're a special treat! It's so cold there that the ground is almost always frozen below the surface, which makes it really difficult for most trees and plants to grow. But luckily for our reindeer pals, they LOVE to eat reindeer moss! Imagine a soft carpet of hundreds of tiny, squishy, antler-shaped branches. Reindeer moss grows all over the Arctic tundra and doesn't mind the cold one bit.

And reindeers' feet are specially designed to help them dig for their dinner. They have four big toes that spread out really wide to help balance their weight, so they don't sink into the soft snow. In the winter, the soft pads under their big toes draw back, creating a space under their sharp-edged hooves. This turns their hooves into a kind of spade that can crack the ice and scoop away the layer of snow, so they can get to the reindeer moss growing on the ground.

?

DID YOU KNOW . . .

The word caribou comes from Mi'kmaq, a native language spoken in the north of Canada and the USA. The Mi'kmaq word *qalipu* translates to 'snow shoveller'!

HOW DO REINDEER STAY WARM?

A reindeer can live in temperatures of -40°C. That's about twice as cold as your freezer at home! Thankfully, they have special thick fur to help them stay warm.

LIKE ME!

When it's cold outside, you might put a big, thick coat on. Your coat traps the air that has been warmed by your body and this keeps you warm as part of a process called **insulation**. Reindeer fur works in a similar way. It's made up of two layers of hair: fine hair at the bottom and hollow hair on top. Each strand of hollow hair is filled with tiny holes, a bit like a sponge. These little holes trap warm air that has been heated by the reindeers' bodies, keeping it close to their skin. It's a brilliant insulator and helps keep them cosy.

DO REINDEER REALLY HAVE RED NOSES?

Rudolf is famous for his bright red nose, but your average reindeer won't parade around with a glowing schnozzle. Regular reindeer have furry noses that are so soft you want to reach out and give them a boop. (I don't actually recommend booping a reindeer on the nose. I'm not sure they'd like it very much.) As well as being super soft, their noses are also brilliant at staying warm!

The tip of a reindeer's nose is packed with tiny blood vessels called capillaries. These carry a constant flow of warm blood that helps keep their nose at the same toasty temperature no matter how cold it is outside. Sometimes the warm blood flows so close to the surface of their skin that the tip of their nose can get a pink, rosy look about it. So perhaps there is a scientific reason behind Rudolf's red nose after all!

DID YOU KNOW ...

Rudolf and the rest of the gang are all female reindeer! Both male and female reindeer grow a pair of antlers that falls off every year so they can grow back larger. Male reindeer usually drop their antlers in the autumn, while females keep their antlers through the winter. Father Christmas's reindeer are usually shown sporting antlers in December, so they must all be females!

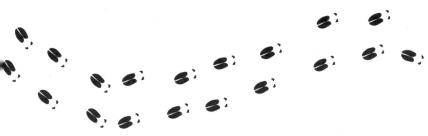

HOW FAR CAN REINDEER REALLY TRAVEL?

It's no surprise Father Christmas picked reindeer to pull his sleigh around the world, as they are brilliant long-distance travellers! Every year, herds of reindeer go on an epic journey in search of places where it's warmer and safer to have their babies. This type of animal movement is called **migration**. Some reindeer migrate a whopping 3,100 miles, which is the furthest ANY land mammal will travel in a single year. That's like walking from the top of Scotland to the bottom of England five-and-a-bit times!

HOW DO REINDEER TALK?

OK, reindeer can't actually talk (except for maybe the magical ones belonging to Father Christmas). But regular reindeer need to be able to find each other in a snow blizzard, so how do they communicate?

Well, you might be surprised to find out that reindeer make a loud clicking sound when they walk. The click is made by a special tendon, which is basically a stretchy band that connects muscle to bone. Every time a reindeer takes a step, the tendon slips and snaps over a bone in the back of one of its feet, making a loud

CLICK!

When a herd of reindeer moves together, they make a LOT of noise. In the spring, reindeer can form super herds of up to 500,000 animals. Just imagine the racket! It would sound like 500,000 ticking clocks or 500,000 light switches turning on and off, or 500,000 people all typing on a keyboard at the same time . . . you get the idea.

But this clicky commotion is really useful because even in the thickest snowstorm, reindeer can still hear the rest of their herd and stay safe as a group. Perhaps we should give this special communication a name:

WHATSSNAP?
CLICKTOK?
SNAPCHAT?

(Oh wait. That's already a thing)

What do you call a reindeer with no eyes?

No Eye Deer.

Father Christmas
Santa's Grotto
Reindeerland
XM4 5HQ

Have you ever sent a letter to Father Christmas? Maybe it looked a bit like this? I always made sure to write my Christmas list in my best handwriting, with my address clearly written at the top (I didn't want my presents ending up in the wrong place!). Sometimes I posted my letter in a postbox; other years, I would put it in the fireplace and the next morning it would be gone! It's a mystery how all our letters manage to reach Father Christmas, but what we do know is that he lives somewhere near the North Pole.

The North Pole is a smart choice for Father Christmas's secret headquarters because it's extremely hard for humans to get to. But where exactly is it, and what makes it such a tricky place to explore?

To understand where the North Pole is, we have to picture Earth as if we are looking at it from space. Our planet is always turning – or spinning – round an imaginary line that passes right through its centre. That imaginary line is called the axis and Earth rotates round it like a spinning top. If the axis were a solid rod and we went to the place where it pushed through the top of the planet, we would find ourselves at the North Pole.

It's called the North Pole because it is the most northern point of Earth. In fact, if you were to stand at the exact point of the North Pole, every direction you turned towards would be south!

The reason why the North Pole makes such a perfect hidden location for Father Christmas's workshop is because it moves all the time. There's no land at the North Pole – instead, it sits in the Arctic Ocean on frozen seawater. This sea ice is about 1 to 3 metres thick, and it slowly moves with the water below it. So if you painted a big red **X** on the ice at the exact point of the North Pole, over time that **X** would drift away from the starting point and no longer be on the exact North Pole any more!

The amount of ice surrounding the North Pole also changes. During the winter, the Arctic sea ice grows to be about the size of the United States, but in the summer, when the Sun is stronger, about half of the ice melts away. However, the amount of Arctic sea ice remaining at the end of summer is getting smaller every year.

THE EFFECTS OF CLIMATE CHANGE

Throughout Earth's history, there have been times when the climate has been much hotter or much colder than it is now. But in the past few hundred years, this kind of change to Earth's climate has been caused by human activity, such as burning fossil fuels like coal and oil. The gases produced by burning fossil fuels go into our atmosphere and trap heat from the Sun in a process called **global warming**. One of the effects of this process is that sea ice is melting faster than ever before. Melting sea ice causes a rise in sea levels, which can result in flooding in other parts of the world. Animals like polar bears – who live and hunt for their food on the ice – are also at risk of losing their homes.

The melting, moving sea ice makes it very difficult for humans to explore, so we have to use helicopters and powerful ships designed to break through the ice to help scientists get to the North Pole.

WHO DISCOVERED THE NORTH POLE?

Many brave explorers have tried to reach the North Pole, but it's hard to say who got there first . . .

1908

The first person who claimed to have reach the North Pole was American doctor and explorer Frederick Albert Cook, who travelled with a team of Inuit guides, a pack of sled dogs and a collapsible boat in case they got cut off by the ice. Cook said he'd made it all the way to the Pole, but he couldn't prove it and some of his teammates disagreed with him . . . how awkward.

1909

American explorer Robert Peary was a former shipmate of Cook's who later became his bitter rival in their race to reach the North Pole. Peary's team included African American explorer Matthew Henson and four Inuit guides named Egingwah, Ooqueah, Ootah and Seeglo. When newspapers reported Cook's earlier discovery of the Pole, Peary did his best to disprove Cook's claim. But neither explorer had any solid proof – and some newspapers even ran a poll to see who the public believed more!

1925

The first expedition to the North Pole that we can be absolutely sure of was made by Norwegian explorer Roald Amundsen. Amundsen and his team didn't use a special ship or dogsleds to cross the ice – he flew over the pole on an airship called *The Norge*!

But if all these icy obstacles weren't enough, let's not forget that the North Pole is really flipping cold! In the UK, the temperature rarely drops below 0ºC. But at the North Pole it can be -40ºC in the winter. MINUS FORTY! A bobble hat and some gloves would NOT be enough. Arctic explorers have to wear lots of special layers to help them survive the harsh climate. Yikes. No wonder Father Christmas wears an enormous furry coat. I wonder if his big beard helps keep his face warm?

So, the North Pole is at the very top of the planet and sits on melting, moving sea ice. You have to fly or use special ships to get there, and it's so cold in the winter that you have to wear enough layers to make you look like an abominable snowman (no offence, Nigel). It's no wonder we haven't found Father Christmas's workshop. He and Mrs Christmas sure picked a faraway but fascinating place to live!

HOW DO ANIMALS STAY WARM IN THE ARCTIC?

We know by now that the North Pole is an extremely challenging environment for humans, but what about other animals? Earlier, we found out how reindeer stay warm on the Arctic tundra (flip back to page 65 if you missed it). Polar bears have a similar type of fur to reindeer that helps keep them warm on the sea ice too. But what about Arctic animals that spend most of their time in and out of the icy water?

Walruses, seals and . . .

PENGUINS?!

SORRY PUDDLES, THERE AREN'T ANY PENGUINS IN THE ARCTIC. YOU ONLY FIND PENGUINS LIVING IN THE ANTARCTIC, WHERE IT'S EVEN COLDER!

What's a penguin's favourite relative?

Aunt Arctica!

Where were we? Oh yes. Walruses, seals and whales such as the narwhal (the unicorn of the sea!) all share a special way of keeping warm, and it has a brilliantly funny name.

BLUBBER!

PSST. PUDDLES. DID YOU KNOW THAT EMPEROR PENGUINS HAVE BLUBBER TOO? TRY SAYING IT FAST!

BLUBBERBLUBBERBLUBBERBLUBBERBLUBBERBLUBBER!

Blubber is a really thick layer of fat between an animal's skin and its muscle. It isn't like the fat we have in our bodies – blubber is much thicker. Walruses can have a layer of blubber about 10cm thick, but the most blubber-riffic animal of them all is the bowhead whale, which can have 43–50cm of blubber round its body!

? DID YOU KNOW ...

For hundreds of years, blubber was a key part of the diet of the Inuit people who live in the Arctic. Blubber is high in energy and a good source of vitamin C, which is hard to find in cold environments as vitamin-C-producing plants (like oranges) can't grow there.

BLUBBER GLOVES

This fun experiment will allow you to feel just how brilliant blubber is at keeping animals warm!

You will need

- a bowl or a sink
- cold water and ice cubes
- two reusable freezer bags (or medical gloves)
- fat (such as lard or butter) or petroleum jelly
- a towel (because this might get messy!)

Make sure you ask permission from your Big Elf before you get busy with blubber and icy water.

In this experiment, you are going to put your hands in cold water. One hand will be bare and the other will be covered in homemade 'blubber'. Which do you think will feel colder and why? Make your best guess and let's get started!

Instructions

1 Fill a bowl with cold water and ice cubes. We can pretend this is the Arctic Ocean.

2 Half fill one of the freezer bags with fat or petroleum jelly. This is our homemade blubber.

3 Place the second bag over your hand – like a glove – and push it into the blubber bag. (This way you don't have to get your hand messy and covered in greasy stuff!)

GREAT WORK. YOU MADE A BLUBBER GLOVE!

4 Use your spare hand to squidge and press the 'blubber' through the bags so your hand has an even coat all around it.

5 Next, dunk both your bare hand and your hand in the blubber glove into the bowl of ice water at the same time. How do they feel?

Your bare hand will feel very cold, while your hand in the blubber glove will feel warmer. This is because blubber is a brilliant insulator. The thick layer of blubber traps your body heat inside the glove and stops it from escaping into the icy water around it. It's a bit like wearing a super-thick wetsuit on your hand!

Your blubber glove will probably only be 1cm-or-so thick, but do you remember how thick bowhead whale blubber can be? 50cm! No wonder they are so happy and comfortable in the cold Arctic waters.

HOW ARE SNOWFLAKES MADE?

Every year, I dream of a white Christmas. Imagine waking up on Christmas morning and realizing . . .

But wait a moment!

Playing in the snow is lots of fun, but have you ever caught a single snowflake and had a closer look? They are beautiful, like tiny, six-pointed pieces of icy art! But how is a snowflake made and where exactly does it come from?

Snowflakes start life in a similar way to rain because they are both part of the **water cycle**.

When water from our oceans, seas and rivers gets heated by the Sun, some of that water turns from a liquid into a gas called **water vapour**. We call this **evaporation**.

Water vapour rises high into the air, where it cools down and then turns from a gas back into tiny droplets of water. We call this **condensation**.

YOU CAN SEE CONDENSATION HAPPENING IF YOU BREATHE ON TO A COLD WINDOW — LITTLE WATER DROPLETS WILL FORM ON THE GLASS!

The tiny droplets of water in the sky bump and clump together, building up and up until they make a cloud! When enough water has condensed, the droplets get really heavy, so they fall down to the ground as rain. The rainwater will eventually find its way back to rivers and oceans, and the cycle starts again.

However, sometimes it can be SO cold in the clouds that when water vapour cools down, it doesn't condense – it freezes! This is when snowflakes are made.

YAY, WE MADE SNOWFLAKES!

HANG ON. It's not quite that simple. For water vapour to freeze and make a snowflake, the water vapour needs something to attach to. Luckily, there are lots of tiny dust particles floating about in the sky.

When water vapour meets a particle of dust in very cold conditions, it will coat the particle and freeze into a tiny crystal of ice. We call this a **seed crystal** because it is the 'seed' from which the rest of the snowflake can grow! As the seed crystal bumps around in the clouds, more and more freezing water vapour will attach to it until it grows into a beautiful ice crystal that we call a snowflake.

Just like rain, when snowflakes become too heavy, they fall to the ground, where they will eventually melt and continue the water cycle.

What do you call an old snowman?

Water.

Have you heard that no two snowflakes are exactly alike? It's true! Each snowflake forms in a different place in the clouds, at a slightly different temperature, surrounded by different amounts of water. So each one will grow completely differently. But how do snowflakes come to look so pretty and delicate?

The particles that make water look a bit like the letter V. This V structure means that when enough frozen water particles have attached themselves to a seed crystal, they naturally make six-sided shapes called **hexagons**. The more water vapour there is in the air, the more complicated the snowflake's shape will be.

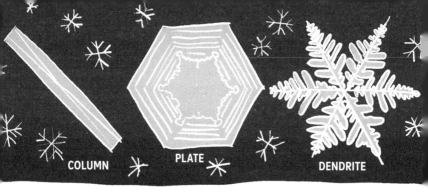

COLUMN   PLATE   DENDRITE

Snowflakes that grow at around -5 to -10°C make **columns**, which look like – unsurprisingly – little icy columns.

The hexagon snow crystal is big, flat and grows between -10 and -20°C. We call these **plates**.

Dendrites have the classic snowflake shape you see on Christmas cards, and form in -20 to -25°C. Their name means 'tree-like' because of their complicated branches.

The path a snowflake takes as it falls from the sky will also change depending on things like the temperature and the wind. No two snowflakes will ever take exactly the same journey, which is another reason they always look different!

So, the next time you play in the snow, why not scoop up a handful of snowflakes and take a closer look to see just how beautiful and unique they are?

FIZZY SNOWMEN!

Do you want to make a snowman? We can all dream, but the chances of getting a white Christmas are quite slim for some of us (especially if you live in Australia, where it's summertime). Not to worry! I've found a way for us all to play with snow no matter where you live.

(OK, so this might not be REAL snow, but it looks like snow, moulds like snow and it fizzes into a magical gloopy mess!)

You will need

- **3 cups of bicarbonate of soda**
- **a mixing bowl**
- **half a cup of white hair conditioner**
- **a tray**
- **crafty bits such as beads, googly eyes, ribbon and paper to decorate your snowman!**
- **a baster, pipette or teaspoon**
- **white vinegar**

Instructions

Make sure you ask permission from your Big Elf before you start. Fake snow can be just as messy as the real stuff!

1 Tip the bicarbonate of soda into your mixing bowl.

2 Drizzle the conditioner into the bicarbonate of soda and mix it with your hands (this is the really messy bit).

3 Keep adding conditioner till you have a crumbly dough. The final mix should hold its shape, just like snow! (If the mixture becomes too wet and sloppy, add a little more bicarbonate of soda.)

4 Pour your fake snow on to the tray.

5 Shape the snow into different-sized snowballs and stack them to make snowmen.

6 Decorate the snowmen with crafty bits. You could use beads for eyes and buttons, some ribbon for a scarf, and some paper to make a carrot nose.

Keep playing with your fake snow, or take this activity to the next level and make your snowmen fizz!

7 Using a baster, pipette or a teaspoon, gently pour the vinegar over the top of your snowmen and watch them fizz and 'melt' away into a gooey puddle.

BONUS IDEAS!

There are LOTS of ways you can make this activity even COOLER! (See what I did there?) Here are a few ideas.

- **Put your fake snow in a sealed container and pop it in the freezer for a few hours. It will feel cold, just like real snow!**

- **Mix a few drops of peppermint essence into the snow mixture to make it smell like candy canes.**

- **Add a few drops of blue food colouring to the vinegar to make your snowman fizz in frosty shades of blue.**

- **Who says you have to make a snowman! Why not make a snow dog? Or a snow snake? Or use cookie cutters to make other snow shapes!**

THE SCIENCE BIT –
WHY DOES VINEGAR MAKE
THE SNOWMEN FIZZ?

Have you ever tasted vinegar? It's kind of sour, a bit sharp and makes your lips scrunch up like a little raisin. This is because vinegar is an **acid**. Lemon juice, fizzy drinks and even milk are also types of acid.

On the other hand, the bicarbonate of soda is an **alkali**, which is basically the opposite of an acid. Cleaning products like bleach, soap and washing powder are also alkalis. (Although it's very important not to taste ANY of these things. They'll taste gross and could make you very poorly.)

When acids and alkalis are by themselves they don't do much, but when they are mixed together, an exciting chemical reaction happens and they become something new!

When the alkaline snowmen are sprinkled with acidic vinegar, the chemical reaction between them makes carbon dioxide gas. It's this gas that makes the fizzy bubbles that we see and hear.

WHY ARE THE DAYS SO SHORT AT CHRISTMAS TIME?

Every year in the run-up to Christmas, I guarantee you will overhear a grown-up saying something along the lines of,

SINCE WHEN DID IT GET DARK SO EARLY?

I CAN'T BELIEVE IT'S THIS DARK AT 3 P.M.!

I'm not exactly sure why they always act so surprised. I mean, it does happen every year – what else do they expect?

OK, so the next time a grown-up makes another comment about how dark it is, here's how you can answer them. First, we have to zoom out again and look at Earth from space.

Can you see that it's not quite straight? It looks like it's been tipped on its side. We learned earlier that Earth rotates around an invisible line called an axis, but it does this on a slight angle and the reason why is seriously cool!

A long, long time ago (like billions of years ago), scientists believe that something MASSIVE crashed into Earth and knocked it over, making it a bit skew-whiff. Now, this is only a theory (which is like a really good, educated guess) but they think that the massive thing that crashed into Earth might have been . . . another planet! And the smash was so intense that it caused a huge chunk of Earth to break off and go on to become our Moon.

The reason we get seasons and different amounts of sunlight throughout the year is because of Earth's slight wonkiness. Our planet makes one full trip around the Sun every year and during this epic journey there are times when some parts of Earth tilt towards the Sun, which means longer, sunnier days for the people who live there. At other times, the same part of Earth will tilt away from the Sun, which means shorter, darker days.

When your part of the planet tilts *towards* the Sun, do you think it is summer or winter?

Thats right! Summer. This means that when the part of the planet you live in tilts *away* from the Sun, it's winter.

To help us talk about different parts of Earth, we can draw an imaginary line around the planet's centre. (Yes, yes I know. ANOTHER imaginary line!) This line wraps round the middle of the planet like Father Christmas's belt! We call it the equator and it splits Earth into two equal halves – the top half is the **Northern Hemisphere** and the bottom half is the **Southern Hemisphere**.

When the Northern Hemisphere is tilted towards the Sun, the Southern Hemisphere is tilted away. This means it is winter in the Northern Hemisphere and summer in the Southern Hemisphere *at the same time.*

It also explains why people in Australia can celebrate Christmas Day with a barbeque on the beach. When it is winter in the Northern Hemisphere, countries in the Southern Hemisphere such as Australia, New Zealand, South Africa and Argentina are all enjoying a lovely hot summer!

The North Pole only has two seasons: winter and summer. Because the North Pole is right at the very top of our planet, it either tilts very close to or very far away from the Sun. This means that for six months of summer, the Sun never sets and for the six months of winter, the Sun never rises!

WHY DO WE HAVE A WINTER SOLSTICE?

You might remember from chapter one that the winter solstice is the shortest day and longest night of the whole year and is usually on 21 or 22 December. But what causes it? Well, the winter solstice happens when the Northern Hemisphere is tilted as far away from the Sun as it possibly can be, so very little sunlight will reach the top half of Earth.

Short, dark days can feel like a bit of a drag in the winter, but the good news is that after the winter solstice, the days start to get longer again as the Northern Hemisphere tilts back towards the Sun. This continues until the **summer solstice**, which is the longest day and shortest night of the year, when the Northern Hemisphere is tilted as close to the Sun as possible.

Of course, the tilty-ness of our planet means that when the Northern Hemisphere is experiencing winter solstice, the Southern Hemisphere will be enjoying summer solstice and vice versa!

MADDIE'S WINTER SOLSTICE FACT FILE

You might remember from chapter one that the Romans celebrated the winter solstice. But did you know that many ancient cultures around the world also celebrated this change from winter into spring? These festivals go by different names, but they all welcome the return of the Sun and longer, warmer days. Here are just a few of them:

YULE

Yule is an ancient pagan celebration that has inspired many of our modern Christmas traditions. Pagans are people with lots of different spiritual beliefs, but they are all connected by their love and respect for nature. Yule celebrates the coming of spring, so many people will decorate with symbols of nature, such as evergreen plants like holly and mistletoe (sound familiar?).

A slightly more unexpected Yule tradition is . . . the Yule Goat! As part of Yule celebrations, towns and cities throughout Sweden build GIANT statues of goats made from straw. The tradition is thought to have been inspired by a group of pagans who worshipped Thor, the god of thunder, lightning and farming, whose chariot was pulled by two goats.

In Sweden, the Yule Goat is so popular that it has become part of many people's Christmas traditions and is often thought of as a gift-giver alongside Father Christmas.

YALDA

Yalda is an ancient Persian festival that is celebrated in Iran and nearby countries like Afghanistan, Tajikistan and Azerbaijan. *Yalda* is a Persian word that means 'birth', so it can symbolize the 'birth' of the Sun after a long winter. Families get together, light candles, read poetry and enjoy a huge feast to get them through the longest night of the year. An important symbol of the festival is the pomegranate, which represents new life and is believed to protect against winter illnesses.

TOJI

In Japan, the winter solstice is called Toji, and many of its traditions are about driving away the cold. One of these warming traditions is having a hot bath scented with yuzu – a citrus fruit that looks a bit like a lemon. It gives the bath a zesty smell and is supposed to be great at fighting off winter illnesses.

But it's not just humans who enjoy a yuzu bath – capybaras love them too! In case you haven't seen one, a capybara is a large rodent that looks a bit like a guinea pig crossed with a beaver. In the 1980s, one Japanese zoo had the idea of giving their capybaras a yuzu bath for Toji. Since then, the yuzu-loving capybaras have gone viral. They look SO adorable!

WHY IS HOLLY SPIKY?

Christmas trees aren't the only types of trees that we use to decorate at Christmas. Have you ever seen a holly tree? It has dark-green glossy leaves and bright red berries.

Just like Christmas trees, holly trees are evergreen, because even when it's cold and snowy outside, holly trees keep their leaves. It's the reason why people love to use holly for Christmas decorations – it adds a bright pop of red and green to wintery days.

Where does Mistletoe go to become famous?

'Holly' wood!

Holly might be the perfect choice for festive decorations but it's not the easiest plant to work with. If you've ever touched it, then you'll know you have to be careful – its leaves are VERY spiky! But have you ever thought to wonder why?

It turns out there is a very good reason why holly has such prickly leaves. The sharp, pointy spikes help the tree protect itself from animals that might try to eat it. When an animal comes along looking for lunch, it sees those spikes (and maybe even gets a little prick on its nose!) then decides to find a less pointy plant to eat instead. This helps the holly tree stay safe, so it can keep growing big and strong.

The spikes act like the holly tree's suit of armour, defending it from danger. This is why we call holly leaves' spikes a type of **defence mechanism**.

But if you take a look at some holly leaves from high up in a tree and compare them to the leaves at the bottom, you might see that they look a little different. Leaves at the top of a holly tree are often smooth and completely prickless! Why do you think that is?

Scientists think it's because a holly tree only needs its spiky defence weapons on the leaves where wild animals like deer and goats might nibble them. Leaves that are high up are already out of harm's way, so they don't need the same spiky tools. These special leaves are a great example of **adaptation**, which is when a plant or animal becomes better suited to survive in its environment over time. Clever, isn't it?

While some animals will learn to keep away from holly leaves, other animals will seek them out, especially in the winter months. Holly leaves are very slow to break down, so their fallen leaves build up into deep piles on the ground. This makes the perfect spot for hedgehogs to snuggle up and build their nests. In the winter, hedgehogs need to slow down, rest and sleep a lot. This is called **hibernation** and it helps them to save energy, so they can survive in the colder months when food is hard to find. The dry fallen holly leaves are like a big, cosy bed for a hedgehog, and the prickly green ones on the tree make a spiky fort, protecting them from danger!

And hedgehogs aren't the only animal to use holly. Many bird species nest in its branches, using its spiky leaves for protection. Blackbirds, fieldfares, redwings and thrushes also like to eat the red berries. One type of bird called the mistle thrush loves the berries of a holly tree so much that it will find a tree and guard it throughout the winter to stop other birds from eating them. (A bit like how your nan might guard the tin of Quality Street on Christmas Day and before you know it all the toffee pennies are gone . . .)

Holly's green leaves and red berries make the perfect choice for Christmas decorations, but as you can tell, they also have a really important purpose in nature. So next time you see a holly wreath or decoration, remember that it's not just pretty and festive, it's also one of nature's winter heroes!

WHY DO PEOPLE KISS UNDER THE MISTLETOE?

Another popular plant we decorate with at Christmas is mistletoe – a spindly green plant with white berries. You might have noticed that grown-ups have a gross habit of kissing when they come close to it. So watch out if anyone catches you under a hanging branch, as you might end up with a slobbery smooch on the cheek!

But where does this weird tradition come from? Well, as with a lot of festive history, we don't exactly know the answer. It's thought that in the UK, kissing under the Christmas mistletoe started in the 1700s and became popular in the Victorian times. But in other countries like France, mistletoe is often linked to New Year and is sometimes given as a good-luck charm for the year ahead.

For centuries, mistletoe has also been connected to love, fertility and new life. The Celtic druids (an ancient type of priest who lived in parts of the UK and Ireland) believed that mistletoe had life-giving powers, as it grew all throughout the winter. And in Norse mythology, mistletoe appears in the myth of Baldr, whose mother Frigg cried tears of joy when he was brought back from the dead. In some versions of the story, Frigg's tears became the white berries of the plant.

So mistletoe's historical connection to love and new beginnings may have something to do with why it's now the symbol for a smooch-fest.

But the idea of mistletoe being 'romantic' is actually quite funny, because mistletoe has a stinky secret. This clever plant is **parasitic**, which means it grows on other plants and steals their water and nutrients to survive. And the way that mistletoe spreads from plant to plant is through POO! Birds eat the berries of the mistletoe plant, and then fly to another tree, where they might leave a number two. The seeds of the mistletoe plant, which have gone through the bird's digestive system and ended up in their droppings, can then spread to the new tree. Hundreds of years ago, people noticed that mistletoe often sprung up near where birds did their business and gave it an appropriate name: 'mistletoe' comes from the Anglo-Saxon words *mistel*, meaning 'dung' and *tan*, meaning 'stick' – so mistletoe literally means POO ON A STICK! That's certainly not something I'd like to be kissed under . . .

BIRDSEED CAKES

Apart from plants that live all year round, like holly and mistletoe, many plants and trees are bare during the cold winter months, and it can be hard for birds to find natural food sources like insects and berries. So why not help some garden birds by giving them the gift of a festive feast?

This cookie-cutter bird cake recipe is perfect for winter because it's packed with high-fat foods like lard and nuts, which will give the birds lots of energy to help them stay warm and active throughout the winter months.

You will need

- suet or lard and a knife
- birdseed
- a mixing bowl and a spoon
- cookie cutters (I like to use stars and gingerbread men for Christmas!)
- scissors
- cut-up paper straws
- a baking tray lined with clingfilm or greaseproof paper
- string or ribbon

This recipe works best with two-parts dry ingredients to one-part fat (the suet or lard). Make as much as you need for as many bird cakes as you'd like!

Instructions

Make sure you ask permission from your Big Elf (a grown-up) before you get to work in the kitchen. Making bird cakes can get messy . . .

1 Warm the suet or lard till it goes squidgy and then cut it into small pieces.

2 Mix the suet or lard and bird seed together in a bowl.

3 Use a spoon (or your hands!) to fill your cookie cutters with the sticky mixture.

4 Make a hole in the mixture and pop pieces of straw through it.

5 Pack a little more seed mixture into the cookie cutters so the straws are tightly held in place.

6 Place the cookie cutters on your lined baking tray and pop them in the fridge for a few hours to set.

7 Once the bird cakes are hard, remove them from the cookie cutters. Then loop a piece of string or ribbon through the straw hole and tie it in a knot.

8 Ask a Big Elf to help you hang your cookie-cutter bird cakes in the garden and wait for the birds to fly over for their Christmas lunch. If you don't have your own garden, don't worry – maybe you could hang them in a relative's garden or a local green space instead?

(And if you have cats in your neighbourhood, try to hang the bird cake somewhere high up where the birds can seek shelter quickly.)

WHAT'S INSIDE A PINECONE?

I love going on wintery woodland walks at Christmas time and finding natural treasures that I can turn into decorations. One thing you can often find scattered on the floor of parks and woodlands is pinecones! In the UK, pinecones grow on all sorts of fir and pine trees, but one of the most common is the Scots pine. Their pinecones drop in the autumn, so you can usually find them among the fallen pine needles and crunchy leaves all the way through to the end of winter.

What do you get when you cross a pinecone and a polar bear?

A fur tree!

Have you ever held a pinecone? I think they look like dragon eggs with all those tough woody scales on the outside! But have you ever wondered what's inside one? And why do they fall from trees in the first place?

If you've ever collected pinecones, you may have noticed that sometimes the scales are wide open and sometimes they are closed tight. Each scale on the outside of the pinecone works like a little door, hiding a tiny seed inside. That door can either be open – letting the seed fly away – or locked shut to keep the seed safe inside. So maybe pinecones are more like magical treasure chests than dragon's eggs?

Once a pine seed has been released from its secret hiding place, it needs to find a place with plenty of light and water for it to grow. Unlike humans, who need lots of help from grown-ups when we are little, seeds don't tend to grow well under their parent plant. Imagine a pine seed dropping out of a pinecone and trying to grow beneath the branch it fell from. The parent tree would block the sunlight, and its big roots would soak up most of the nearby water. That's why many seeds, like pine seeds, have adapted to travel far away to grow.

The seeds inside a pinecone have a special shape – they look a bit like wings! When the wind blows, it catches the seed's wing and carries it far away from the parent tree, where it will have a better chance of growing.

But there are lots of potential dangers that could make the seed's journey difficult. If it gets wet, it will become heavy and the wind won't carry it very far. And if the ground is frozen, the seed won't break through to the soil where it can grow. So on cold and rainy days, pinecone scales close up and lock their seeds inside, so they don't get wasted. When the weather is dry again, the scales open up and the seeds can be whisked away by the wind to a sunny spot where they can grow into healthy plants.

You can test a pinecone at home with a curious experiment. Find two pinecones that look the same, then put one in a glass of water and one somewhere dry and warm. Leave them for a day and see what happens. The pinecone in water should close up and the one that's dry will be open!

So, pinecones change with their environment to keep seeds safe. What a cool adaptation! But did you know that it's only *female* pinecones that make seeds? There are also male pinecones that look a bit different to the woody, scaly female ones. Male pinecones are soft and spongy, and instead of seeds they produce **pollen**, which is like a dusty powder. When male pinecones release their pollen, it's carried through the air by the wind and will hopefully fall on a female pinecone on a different pine tree. If this happens, the pine seeds tucked away in the female pinecone will be **pollinated**, which means they can grow into baby trees!

SNOWY OWL PINECONES

Pinecones are also perfect for Christmas crafts – they look fantastic hanging from a tree, covered with glitter, or made into Christmassy characters. Here's how you can transform one into an adorable snowy owl! The brown pinecone scales help recreate the dark, brownish markings that snowy owls have on their feathers.

You will need

- a roll of cotton wool
- a dry pinecone
- white, yellow and black felt (or card)
- scissors
- a black pen
- PVA glue
- googly eyes (optional)
- string/ribbon

Instructions

Make sure you ask a Big Elf to be on stand-by to help you with the scissors.

1. Pull apart some of the cotton wool into small pieces and stuff them into the pinecone. It helps to poke the cotton wool between the scales, so it fits snugly. Keep going till the pinecone is fluffy all over!

2. Glue two tightly rolled pieces of cotton wool to the base of the pinecone. These are the snowy owl's feet.

3. Ask a Big Elf to help you cut two wings from the white felt, then use the black pen to draw on a feather pattern.

4. Cut two small circles from the yellow felt to make the eyes, and a small beak from the black felt.

5. Glue the wings, beak and eyes on to the pinecone.

6. Finish the eyes by drawing a black dot (or adding some googly eyes) in the centre of the yellow circles.

7. If you want, you could tie a piece of string to the top of the pinecone and hang your snowy owl as a wintery decoration!

THE SCIENCE BIT –
SNOWY OWLS IN NATURE

Snowy owls get their name from their snow-white feathers and the cold Arctic places they live in. Just like lots of the Arctic animals we've learned about, snowy owls have adapted to survive icy temperatures. They have tightly packed feathers that trap warm air close to their body, and soft fluffy feathers on their feet that help stop them from sinking into the snow.

? DID YOU KNOW . . .

Not all owls are night hunters. Some owls, such as the snowy owl, hunt during the daytime too. In the Arctic summer, the Sun never sets, so it's a good job snowy owls don't have to wait for it to get dark before they can eat!

THE CURIOUS CHRISTMAS CREATURE GALLERY!

What do a worm, a sea snail, a wasp, a shrimp, a butterfly and a crab all have in common?

VERY LITTLE?

I can see why you might think that. But there is a surprising link between all of these animals – CHRISTMAS!

When we think of Christmas animals, we usually imagine reindeer and robins, but it turns out there's a whole host of weird and wonderful creatures who have Christmas-themed names. I think it's important to share a little love with all the animals on Earth (even the seriously bizarre ones), so get ready to meet some Christmas characters you've probably NEVER heard of.

Welcome to the Curious Christmas Creature Gallery!

CHRISTMAS TREE WORM

Name: Christmas tree worm (*Spirobranchus giganteus*)
Habitat: Tropical coral reefs
Likes to eat: Microscopic plants and animals

The Christmas tree worm gets its name because it looks like a teeny tiny colourful Christmas tree! They're about 4cm in length and live on tropical reefs around the world.

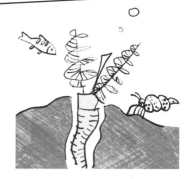

Christmas tree worms have brightly coloured festive crowns that stick out from their tube-like bodies. These crowns are made up of feathery **radioles** that look a bit like the branches of a tree. The radioles are covered in wiggly hairs called **cilia**, which trap bits of food and guide it towards the worm's mouth. They'll happily munch on just about anything, including microscopic plants and animals.

While their festive crowns can be seen on display in the water, most of their wormy bodies are hidden inside their tube-shaped burrow in the coral. (Their favourite type of coral looks like a brain.) If a Christmas tree worm ever feels threatened, it can suck in its fancy crowns and duck down into its burrow, away from danger. To be extra safe, they also have a spiky plug on the end of a long tentacle called an **operculum**. If they need to, they can poke their operculum upwards and block the entrance to their burrow. It's a bit like shutting the door so no one can come in.

STARRY NIGHT CRACKER BUTTERFLY

Name: Starry night cracker butterfly (*Hamadryas laodamia*)
Habitat: Central and South America
Likes to eat: Rotting fruit and animal poo

The starry night cracker butterfly has black wings with a spattering of blue and white spots that look just like a starry sky. The famous painter Vincent van Gogh once created a painting called *Starry Night*, and this is what the butterfly was named after. But what about the 'cracker' part of its name?

It's nothing to do with Christmas crackers, but they are both quite loud! Most male cracker butterflies can make a special noise with their wings that sounds like crackling bacon frying in a pan. The cracking noise is believed to attract female butterflies and scare away any potential predators.

Unlike most butterflies, who use their long, curly tongues to slurp sweet, syrupy nectar from flowers, the starry night cracker prefers stinky food and will be found sucking up the juices from rotting fruit and . . . animal poo! Bleurgh!

SEA ANGEL

Name: Sea angel (*Clione limacina*)
Habitat: Deep sea, worldwide
Likes to eat: Sea butterflies

The sea angel might look like a graceful swimming jelly baby, but don't be fooled! These squidgy sea snails are actually savage hunters.

The sea angel doesn't have a shell but believe me, it is a type of snail. Just like the snails on land, the sea angel has a muscly 'foot' to help it move around. This foot has two wing-like fins called **parapodia** that allow it to glide through the water. The sea angel moves them back and forwards like oars on a boat to help them swim at speeds of 10cm per second – about as fast as a goldfish. Pretty nippy!

Sea angels like to eat another type of sea snail called a sea butterfly. Sea butterflies DO have shells, so the sea angel has developed a terrifying tool hidden in its head to help it gobble them down!

When a sea angel comes across a delicious sea butterfly, it will open its mouth and push out a set of spiky tentacles that are covered in tiny hooks and suction cups. They are called **buccal cones** and the sea angel uses them to reach into the sea butterfly's shell, grab the soft body parts, yank them out and shove them into its mouth. Fairly gory stuff for an animal with such an angelic name.

FAIRYFLY

Name: Fairyfly (Mymaridae)
Habitat: Tropical forests, Costa Rica
Likes to eat: Nectar

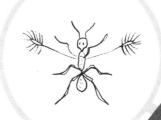

Have you ever seen a fairy? Each year, I put one on top of our Christmas tree, although I've never seen one in real life. But we do know of one real-life fairy – the fairyfly! They're still very hard to spot though as they're SO tiny.

Fairyflies are some of the smallest known insects in the world. One type of fairyfly is *Tinkerbella nana*, which is named after not one, but *two* characters from *Peter Pan*: Tinkerbell, the feisty lovable fairy, and Nana, the loyal dog and housekeeper.

Tinkerbella nana is so small that it's pretty much impossible to see. It's only 250 micrometres long, which is roughly the same as two-and-a-half strands of human hair. In folk tales, fairies are known for being mischievous, but these tiny insects are next-level naughty! Although *Tinkerbella nana* is called a fairyFLY, it's actually a **parasitic wasp**.

Adult females lay their own eggs inside another insect's eggs (THAT'S how small their eggs are!). Her wasp babies will then grow by eating the nutrients from the other egg, killing the other baby insect in the process. They may be tiny, but *Tinkerbella nana* and her family of fairyflies are not to be messed with.

CANDY CANE SHRIMP

Name: Candy cane shrimp (*Alpheus randalli*)
Habitat: Indian and Pacific Oceans
Likes to eat: Marine snow (bits of old plants, animals and poo floating about in the water), as well as small molluscs like mussels

The candy cane shrimp gets its name because it looks like – you guessed it – a red and white candy cane! It might look sweet enough to eat, but don't underestimate the candy cane shrimp. It can throw one of the most powerful punches in the animal kingdom!

They have two claws, one of which is much larger than the other and seriously POWERFUL. It's made of two parts connected by a joint – the top part works like a trigger that can be drawn back, locked in place, and released to snap shut really quickly. When the claw snaps, it makes a wave of bubbles that whoosh out so fast they can stun a small fish or break glass. In fact, the snap is SO powerful that when the bubbles collapse in the water they briefly become hotter than the surface of the SUN! This secret weapon allows the shrimp to stun their prey, but also to communicate.

But candy cane shrimp don't work alone. They have terrible eyesight, so they team up with another ocean creature to help them survive – the Randall's prawn goby! These two animals work together in a way that means they both benefit – we call this a **mutualistic relationship**. The candy cane shrimp helps the goby fish dig a burrow they can both live in, and in return, the goby fish hovers over the shrimp and keeps a lookout to protect them from predators.

CHRISTMAS ISLAND RED CRAB

Name: Christmas Island red crab (*Gecarcoidea natalis*)
Habitat: Christmas Island, Indian Ocean
Likes to eat: Fallen leaves, seedlings, fruits and flowers

Christmas Island sounds like a magical place where Father Christmas goes on holiday, but it's actually a tiny tropical island just off the coast of northern Australia. It's home to a species of colourful crustaceans known for their jaw-dropping journey from land to sea.

Christmas Island red crabs prefer to stay out of the burning, direct sunlight and spend most of the year in the shade of the forests. However, when the rainy season arrives in October, they creep out of their burrows and begin the 5-mile-long journey to their seaside breeding grounds. Over **50 MILLION** bright red crustaceans migrate at the same time, creating a crawling crab carpet that covers the island's roads, beaches, cliffs and forest floors. It's an awesome spectacle!

Is there someone else you can think of who dazzles in red and makes an enormous journey once a year? Oh, wait! Perhaps Father Christmas and the crabs of Christmas Island do have something in common after all?!

What do you call a crab that eats mince pies?

Santa Claws.

MADDIE'S CURIOUS CHRISTMAS QUIZ – ROUND TWO

Ready to sleigh your way through round two? It's time to brush up on your reindeer knowledge and answer the next ten questions about animals and nature.

1. What surprising noise do reindeer make?

2. Is the North Pole on ice or land?

3. Which explorer flew over the North Pole?

4. What do we call the thick layer of fat some Arctic animals have to keep them warm?

5. What type of animal is a sea angel?

6. What do you find in the middle of every snowflake?

7. What surprising thing may have crashed into our planet billions of years ago?

8. If the Northern Hemisphere (the top half of Earth) is tilting towards the Sun, is it summer or winter there?

9. Which animal likes to make a nest under a pile of dry holly leaves?

10. If it is rainy and wet outside, will pinecones be open or closed?

Answers on page 233

FOOD

Christmas dinner might just be the best part of Christmas Day! What do you have for yours? My favourite Christmas food is probably roast potatoes and gravy. One year, my family actually forgot about the roast potatoes and left them in the oven, so we ended up having a roast potato course between our main and dessert! We dunked them in gravy like it was a fondue – yum! Sorry if that's got your mouth watering already, because we're about dip into the delicious history and science of Christmas food . . .

WHY DO WE HAVE TURKEY AT CHRISTMAS?

If I'm being honest, I'm not a massive fan of turkey. If it's not cooked REALLY well it can be quite dry. Some people even soak their bird in a bucket of brine (salty water) for twenty-four hours just to try and get some moisture into it!

Children: This turkey tastes like an old sofa!

Mum: Well, you asked for something with plenty of stuffing!

I'm not saying that turkey can't be delicious, but I know I'm not alone in thinking it's a bit overrated. So how did this giant, gobbling bird become such an important part of a traditional Christmas dinner?

To find out, let's go on a journey through history. We'll start at a medieval banquet, where you won't find a roasted turkey, but a pickled boar's head!

THE WILD WORLD OF MEDIEVAL BANQUETS

In medieval times, Christmas feasts were a luxury that only wealthy people could afford, and they were all about showing off. It wouldn't have been especially unusual to find a goose roasted in garlic, spit-roasted peacocks, beef tongue, fish platters, piles of vegetables, shellfish platters, fish stew, rabbit pie, eel pie and pigeon pie all on the SAME TABLE!

And let's not forget the all-important boar's head centrepiece. And yes, it's as gruesome as it sounds. If Frankenstein held a dinner party, this dish would be his showstopper. Things are about to get icky, so look away if you'd rather skip the recipe for . . .

How to make a medieval boar's head

- Remove the skin from the skull and sew the eyes, nose and mouth shut.
- Pickle the skin in vinegar and spices until chewy.
- Stuff the pickled skin with layers of bacon, spices and breadcrumbs, then seal it up like a meaty balloon.
- Wrap the stuffed head in cloth and boil it with carrots, parsnips and onions before leaving it to simmer for five hours.
- Cool overnight and serve!

The boar's head was so popular, it even came with its own song. 'The Boar's Head Carol' would be sung as the head on a platter was paraded around the table, before being carved up and piled high on to guests' plates in the ultimate display of medieval extravagance.

The boar's head in hands I bring,
with garlands gay & birds singing!
I pray you all to help me sing, who are at this banquet!

Today, we might gasp in horror at the idea, but there is one place where the medieval tradition lives on. Every year on the Saturday before Christmas, Oxford University's The Queen's College puts on the Boar's Head Gaudy, where (you guessed it) pickled boar's head is served and the carol is sung by a choir. However, this might just be the ONLY place where the medieval delicacy is still eaten.

Apparently, it tastes like pork pie, which might make it sound a little more appetizing . . .
OK, maybe not.

?

DID YOU KNOW . . .

People didn't actually use plates in medieval times – they served their food on a slice of bread, or a hollowed-out loaf called a trencher!

But did you notice something missing from the medieval Christmas banquet? That's right – no turkey! Turkeys didn't even arrive in England until the time of the Tudors, when Henry VIII was on the throne.

But where do you think turkeys came from in the first place?

TURKEY . . . ?

Good guess, but . . .

Turkeys are actually from the Americas! Let me explain.

TURKISH TUDOR TURKEYS?

These wobbly faced birds were originally brought to Europe by Spanish sailors who probably discovered them in what is now Mexico, during their exploration of the Americas. Years later, turkeys were introduced to England by a Turkish merchant company, so people assumed the birds were Turkish and named them . . . turkeys. Original, right?

If we followed the same logic, turkeys should actually be called mexicos!

Turkeys immediately became popular with wealthy Tudors because they were meatier than chickens and tastier than some of the other weird birds they'd been eating, like peacocks and blackbirds. Henry VIII himself had one on his Christmas dinner table, making turkeys very trendy in high society. However, they were SO expensive, that most people preferred to eat the cheaper alternative – goose.

VICTORIAN BIRDS IN BOOTS!

Fast-forward to the Victorian times, when turkeys were being farmed in the east of England – especially Norfolk, where the land was perfect for raising them. The challenge was transporting them to London for the rich folk. Some turkeys were loaded on to carriages, but others had to walk! Around 200,000 turkeys made the three-month journey on foot every single year. It was such a long way that some marching birds were even given special leather boots to protect their feet!

You'd think the sight of this feathery festive parade might have inspired more of the public to start eating turkey. But it wasn't until Charles Dickens's classic story *A Christmas Carol* was published in 1843 that turkey truly reached the masses. In the story, a miserable man named Ebeneezer Scrooge learns to love Christmas, and at the end he buys the poor Cratchit family an enormous turkey. The popular story warmed the public's hearts and inspired lots of families to finally give the bird a try!

THE 1930S AND BEYOND

As the popularity of turkeys went up, their price dropped, and by the 1930s, the turkey had finally become the most popular centrepiece of the Christmas table – and the tradition still exists today.

Of course, not EVERYONE eats turkey. Some people prefer a different meat or choose a delicious vegetarian option (I love a nut roast!). And there are plenty of other fantastic festive foods, as we're about to find out in our next question . . .

WHAT DO PEOPLE AROUND THE WORLD EAT FOR CHRISTMAS DINNER?

Christmas is celebrated in different ways around the globe, but there's one thing all our holidays have in common: FOOD! No matter where you live, I bet you have a favourite food that you can't wait to eat. As you know, mine is roast potatoes, but your festive treat of choice might be totally different.

Feast your eyes on these four delicious Christmas dinners that are enjoyed by families all over the world. Be warned: this part may leave you feeling hungry . . .

A FAST-FOOD FAVOURITE IN JAPAN

Even though Christmas isn't a national holiday in Japan, millions of families still get into the Christmas spirit by enjoying . . . a bucket of Kentucky Fried Chicken! KFC has been a Japanese Christmas dinner favourite since 1974, and the whole thing started with a really smart advertising campaign.

Takeshi Okawara, the manager of the first KFC in the country, overheard some American tourists saying how much they missed having turkey on Christmas Day, and he thought that chicken could be a good alternative. So, he came up with a genius idea: the Christmas 'Party Barrel' – a bucket filled with fried chicken.

Before the Party Barrel, there wasn't really a Christmas tradition in Japan. But Okawara's idea quickly filled that gap and became a beloved tradition that families could repeat year after year.

The advertising campaign was so successful that around 3.6 million families now treat themselves to a KFC bucket every year on 25 December. (That's a LOT of fried chicken!) People even place their orders weeks in advance to make sure they can get their hands on one of the special Christmas dinners. The Christmas Party Barrel isn't just full of fried chicken, either: it includes other treats like a chocolate or strawberry cake, and a special Christmas plate to display your food.

It certainly takes the stress out of Christmas Day. But maybe don't suggest to your grown-ups that you'd prefer a fried chicken takeaway over their cooking – it may not go down well.

A FISHY FEAST IN ITALY

Ahoy there, seafood lovers! In the south of Italy and many Italian-American households, one of the most beloved Christmas Eve meals is 'The Feast of the Seven Fishes', also known as *'La Vigilia'*.

As the name suggests, this Christmas Eve feast is typically made up of seven fish dishes. Fried calamari (squid), salted cod, eel, anchovies, scallops, clams, octopus and seafood spaghetti are all popular choices. Lobster tails might even make an appearance if the chef is feeling fancy! It's not just fish though – most families will make some fried or pickled vegetables to go on the side.

But why so many fish, you might ask? Well, it goes back to an old Catholic belief that meat and dairy should be avoided on holy days, such as Christmas Eve. As Italian Catholics couldn't eat meat or use animal products like butter and cheese, they would often eat fish and vegetables fried in olive oil instead. It's hard to know exactly why there are SEVEN fish dishes, but we do know that the number seven is connected with lots of Catholic stories and symbols. In fact, it's so important that the number seven is repeated more than 700 times in the Bible!

Did you hear about the seafood diet?
You see food and you eat it!

A SWIMMING SURPRISE IN SLOVAKIA

Do you like taking nice, relaxing baths? I sure do! Adding bubbles or bath bombs can make it even more fun. But do you know what I definitely would NOT want in my bath? A giant FISH! Can you imagine it? No thank you.

So it might surprise you to learn that some families in central Europe choose to plop a fish in their bathtub in the run-up to Christmas!

You may be wondering why anyone would want a fish in their bath. Well, in countries such as Slovakia, Poland, the Czech Republic and Lithuania, it's traditional to eat a type of fish called a carp as part of Christmas Eve dinner. The Christmas carp is usually caught fresh from a river or a carp farm. But before it can be fried in breadcrumbs and served with soup and potato salad, it needs to swim about in the family bathtub for a couple of days.

A TAMALES TRADITION IN MEXICO

Mexican Christmas is all about coming together and cooking up a storm. For many families, the best part of the festive season is the *tamalada* – a party where everyone gets together to make *tamales*!

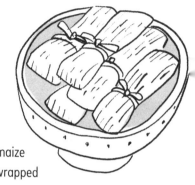

Tamales are tasty parcels made from maize dough, meat, cheese and vegetables, wrapped in a corn husk and steamed to perfection. Today, *tamales* come in all sorts of different flavours, but they've been around for thousands of years. In fact, the tradition of eating *tamales* dates back to the ancient people of Mesoamerica (a historical region that includes parts of Mexico and Central America), such as the Aztecs, Maya and Olmecs.

It's hard to know exactly when *tamales* first appeared, but we do have some incredible archaeological evidence. In a stunning wall painting found in Guatemala, we can see pictures of a Maize god and a kneeling woman holding a basket of *tamales*. The painting probably dates back to 100 BCE (that's more than 2,000 years ago!), but it's likely *tamales* have been part of Mexican culture for even longer.

The painting tells us that *tamales* have always been a special food fit for the gods, and that women were the original *tamale* makers. Generations of women would spend hours cooking and wrapping these delicious treats in their natural packaging. You could say that *tamales* were one of the first portable fast foods – perfect for hunters, travellers, soldiers and families on the move.

Today, Mexican families hold *tamaladas* to bring everyone together in a big celebration. *Tamales* are simple to make, but preparing enough for a feast takes time. So the party becomes a *tamale*-making production line, allowing families to connect and share an age-old tradition. (Although I pity whoever gets lumped with the washing up!)

BITESIZE FACT!

We can also thank the ancient civilizations of Mesoamerica for another favourite Christmas food: CHOCOLATE! Over 4,000 years ago, the Olmecs were the first people to grow cacao plants and turn the beans into a chocolatey drink that they used as medicine. Hundreds of years later, the Mayans thought of hot chocolate as the **drink of the gods**. They preferred it thick and foamy, with a spicy chilli kick. Finally, the Aztecs came along and loved it so much that they even used cacao beans as money. Imagine being able to pay for things with chocolate coins!

So, what do you think of those four festive feasts? And if you could pick one to try, which would you choose?

HOW DO ASTRONAUTS EAT CHRISTMAS DINNER IN SPACE?

Christmas Day as an astronaut on the International Space Station (ISS) must feel pretty strange. Your home is zooming through space at around 17,500 miles per hour; you're at least 220 miles away from the nearest carol concert; and you're definitely outside of Father Christmas's delivery area. But perhaps the biggest challenge for an astronaut on Christmas Day is how to eat your Christmas dinner when **gravity** is so low that the gravy will probably fly up and hit you in the face!

Gravity is an invisible force that acts on things without touching them. On Earth, gravity is what pulls us towards the centre of the planet, keeping our feet firmly on the ground. But on the ISS, where there is reduced gravity, everything floats! Water will fly out of a cup and crumbs can get EVERYWHERE. So scientists needed to develop special ways of packaging and eating foods. Not only does food have to be safe and easy to eat, but it also has to be lightweight, long-lasting and easy to pack so the space station can carry enough for long periods of time.

One way of making food last on long trips to space is by **freeze-drying** it. Freeze-drying is when food is cooked and quickly frozen, and then all the water is sucked out of it, so it becomes crunchy and airy. This makes the food last much longer without being kept in a fridge. Some freeze-dried foods can be eaten dry, but others need to be **rehydrated**. This means adding water to the food to make it edible. So that the liquid doesn't end up flying everywhere, rehydrated foods are sealed in special pouches with taps. Astronauts pour the water into the tap, mix it up, and squeeze the food straight into their mouths through a spout.

For special occasions like Christmas Day, food scientists on Earth plan a holiday menu that is sent to the space station in advance. In the past, astronauts have enjoyed space-friendly versions of traditional Christmas foods such as smoked turkey slices, pouches of sweet potatoes and cranberry sauce, and green beans. And for dessert, the crew were once sent shortbread biscuits with squeezy icing for them to decorate their own Christmas treats!

Another favourite dessert option on the ISS is Christmas pudding – apparently the British astronaut Tim Peake once requested one for his festive meal. Christmas puddings are a good choice for astronauts as they're long-lasting and full of flavour. Which is important, because astronauts often find that their sense of taste becomes really dull in space. On Earth, body fluids like saliva move downwards through the body because of gravity. But in space, these fluids move about in an astronaut's body, creating a feeling similar to a blocked nose that leaves many foods tasting bland. Luckily, Christmas pudding is packed with fruit, nuts and spices, so it might just get astronauts' tastebuds tingling!

One Christmas favourite you won't find on the ISS is the Brussels sprout. Why? Because space agencies avoid serving any food that could make astronauts fart! The gases in farts are flammable, which could be very dangerous in a small capsule in the middle of space, where farts have nowhere to escape to.

Which leads us on to our next question . . .

WHY DO BRUSSELS SPROUTS MAKE YOU FART?

Have you ever tried Brussels sprouts? They're those little leafy green balls that look like baby cabbages. Some people love them, but some people REALLY dislike them.

If you love them, shout, **'YUM!'**

If you think they're gross, shout, **'YUCK!'**

Personally I'm on team YUM. They're *so* good for you and packed with vitamin C! Although they have to be cooked in just the right way to taste good – if they've been boiled for too long, they get really bitter and mushy.

Whether you're on team YUM or team YUCK, there's no denying that sprouts have a habit of making everyone rather . . . gassy. And I'm not talking about a polite little toot. Brussels sprouts can cause some seriously smelly Boxing Day explosions!

But why do these pocket-size veggies make us more likely to drop a stink bomb than other foods?

To find out, first we need to ask the question . . .

WHAT IS A FART?

Quite simply, a fart is the release of gas from your bottom. Some of that gas is air that can sometimes be swallowed when you eat and chew, but most of the gas comes from the food that you eat. When you digest food, your body breaks it down into nutrients that it can use, and gas is produced as a result. If we didn't let one rip occasionally, that gas would build up in our bodies and we would explode! Farts are just a very normal way for all that gas to escape. They can be silent and deadly, or loud like a trumpet, but we all do them. Even the king of England. And your teacher.

But how does our digestive system make all that gas?

HOW ARE FARTS MADE?

Your digestive system is made up of different parts that your food has to travel through on its journey into your mouth, through your body and out of your bum.

The journey starts in your mouth, where your teeth chew up your food and start to break it down into smaller bits.

Next, you swallow, and the munched-up food travels down your **oesophagus** into your stomach, where **digestive juices** packed with **enzymes** break down your food and turn it into sloppy mush!

Digestive juices are fluids made in your stomach and intestines that help digest food. **Enzymes** are special substances that control how fast a chemical reaction happens – for example, how quickly your food is broken down.

Now the mushy, partly digested food can move along into your **small intestine**.

The **small intestine** is like a long tube. It's the longest part of the digestive system and can be up to 10.5 metres long (that's almost the same as measuring six Maddies from head to toe!).

The small intestine squeezes your food along and squirts even more digestive juices on to the mush to make it super watery. This makes it easier for the nutrients from your food to move through the walls of the small intestine, so they can be carried around the rest of your body to be used as fuel.

The leftover, undigested food finishes its journey with a long trip through your large intestine and the colon. We can think of this part as THE FART FACTORY.

The large intestine and colon are full of friendly bacteria that are pretty good at breaking down anything that the digestive juices and special enzymes haven't been able to. But when they do this, the busy bacteria make a lot of gas in the process! Some of these fart gases don't smell bad at all, but others really STINK.

The unsmelly ones
Carbon dioxide, hydrogen and methane
They don't smell, but they are flammable, which is why astronauts need to avoid farting at all costs!

The smelly ones
Hydrogen sulphide reeks of rotten eggs.

Methyl mercaptan smells of mouldy cabbages. It's the same stuff that skunks spray on unwelcome visitors.

All that gas, along with the leftover undigested food (that's poo, by the way), slowly makes its way through your large intestine until it drops into your colon and eventually escapes from your anus (the bit the poo comes out of) in a variety of plops and parps.

So that's how farts are made, but why do Brussels sprouts make us so much fartier than other foods?

WHY DO SPROUTS MAKE YOU SO FARTY?

The foods that make you fartiest tend to be the ones that can't be completely broken down by the enzymes in the digestive juices in your stomach and small intestine. Instead, they journey all the way into the large intestine and colon, where your friendly bacteria get to work and make fart gas in the process!

Sprouts are hard to digest in the stomach and small intestine because they contain a type of sugar called **raffinose**. (Raffinose is also found in cabbages, broccoli and cauliflower, so you might find that those veggies make you parp too!) Raffinose can't be broken down by digestive juices, so it travels to the Fart Factory.

Here, in the large intestine and colon, your friendly bacteria have the right tools to break down the raffinose, but in doing so, they make hydrogen methane and carbon dioxide gas. Those gases make you fart, but they aren't smelly ones. So why do Brussels sprouts give you a serious case of the stinkers?

Well, sprouts are also packed with a type of chemical that contains **sulphur**. Sulphur is super stinky, and it does a good job of putting off animals who might try to eat sprouts in the wild. It's these sulphur-containing chemicals that the bacteria turn into the smelly gases hydrogen sulphide and methyl mercaptan, resulting in a disgustingly eggy, cabbage-y smell!

So the Brussels sprout's combination of raffinose AND sulphur-containing chemicals makes the perfect recipe for massive, smelly farts.

There's nothing we can do to avoid the Christmas chuffs (other than stop eating Brussels sprouts altogether). But if, like me, you think they're rather tasty, maybe just open a window the morning after your Christmas lunch!

BREAK-OUT SPROUTS!

If you're on team YUCK then I have the perfect gift for you. I have designed a Christmas contraption that keeps sprouts LOCKED AWAY to trap those little green monsters. That is, until someone lets them break out!

Whether you like sprouts or not, I'm sure you'll enjoy this hilarious game of skill, nerve and silliness! You can play in a pair or a group, but I warn you, this game gets competitive, and I cannot be held accountable for any Christmas Day squabbles that Break-out Sprouts might cause . . .

You will need

- Brussels sprouts (enough to fill one third of the colander – I find twelve sprouts work well)
- a colander
- pipe cleaners or dry spaghetti
- two piles of books to balance the colander on

The set-up

Make sure you ask permission from your Big Elf before you start playing with the Brussels sprouts. They might be needed for tonight's dinner!

1 Place the sprouts in the bottom of the colander.

2 Thread the pipe cleaners or spaghetti through the holes so they go in one side and out the other.

3 Keep threading the pipe cleaners or spaghetti round the colander, so they crisscross and make a mesh – almost like a prison for the sprouts!

4 Turn the colander upside down and make sure that NO Brussels sprouts fall out!

5 Raise the upside-down colander off the floor or table by resting it on two piles of books (or whatever else you have).

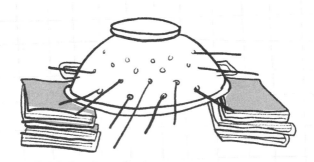

How to play

1 Each player takes a turn at pulling out a pipe cleaner or piece of spaghetti.

2 If any sprouts tumble out of the colander when it's your turn, shout, 'BREAK-OUT SPROUTS!', and keep them to the side in a pile.

3 As the game continues, it will become harder and more nerve-wracking. (This is the REALLY fun bit!)

4 The game ends when all of the sprouts have broken out of the colander.

5 The player who finishes with the fewest sprouts wins!

Once you've played the game, give the sprouts a rinse, and they'll be perfectly OK to eat! (Did you think you could get away with not eating them? Mwahahaha . . .)

If the very sight of Brussels sprouts makes you turn a bit green, then you could use pompoms, ping-pong balls or scrunched-up bits of paper instead.

HOW DO CRANBERRIES GROW?

We eat lots of different types of fruits and vegetables (especially at Christmas), but we rarely stop to think about how they come to be on our plates. What are some plants you like to eat at Christmas, and do you know how they grow?

- **Carrots, parsnips, sweet potatoes and potatoes all grow in soil under the ground.**
- **Brussels sprouts grow on long, thick stalks. (I think they look like a gnarly club for trolls!)**
- **Peas grow inside pods.**
- **Chestnuts grow inside spiky cases that fall from a tree.**

There's another plant we eat at Christmas that grows in a very unique way: the cranberry!

These tiny, round fruits are VERY good for you, but they're super sour, so we mix them with sugar to make them taste sweet and juicy. We use cranberries to make all sorts of yummy treats, like cranberry juice, dried cranberries and cranberry sauce, which is often served with turkey at special holidays like Christmas, or the American holiday Thanksgiving.

Not only are cranberries delicious, but they're also great for decorating. I love to string them into glossy, beaded garlands and drape them around my Christmas tree!

Why did the cranberry turn red?
Because it saw the turkey dressing!

But my favourite thing about cranberries is the way we grow and pick them. Would you believe me if I told you that we take them for a swim in a bog?

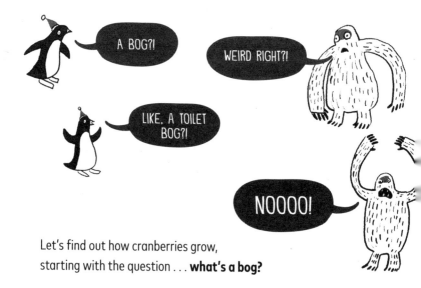

A BOG?!

WEIRD RIGHT?!

LIKE, A TOILET BOG?!

NOOOO!

Let's find out how cranberries grow, starting with the question . . . **what's a bog?**

CRANBERRY BOGS

Cranberries grow on long woody vines that creep along the ground in special wetland habitats called bogs. Wetlands are places where the ground is naturally damp and spongy, but in cranberry bogs farmers deliberately flood the ground with tons of fresh water from nearby lakes. When this happens, the cranberry bogs look like enormous ponds. Some of the world's largest cranberry bogs are found in North America and Canada, and they can be up to 200 acres wide. That's big enough to fit 3,100 tennis courts, or fifteen Windsor Castles inside!

To find out why farmers use such an unusual method to grow their cranberries, let's start at the beginning of the fruit's life cycle . . .

WINTER

In the winter, cranberry vines already have tiny baby buds that are ready to flower and grow into cranberries as soon as spring arrives. These little buds are super sensitive to the cold. This is why cranberry farmers flood the bogs with water – it helps protect the buds through the winter months. The water freezes over, making the bogs look like huge ice-skating rinks! The blanket of water below the ice traps heat, which helps keep the plants warm and protects the buds from freezing while they enjoy a long winter's rest.

SPRING

In the spring, the ice melts and the water is drained back into the lakes surrounding the cranberry bogs. As the weather gets warmer, the tiny buds that have survived the winter will bloom into pretty pink and white flowers, and a second bud will start to grow on the vines. By the end of spring, each vine will carry two buds – the one that will grow into a cranberry this year, and a tiny new bud that will last all the way through until next season. This is why cranberry farmers have to look after cranberry vines so carefully – they are always caring for two years' worth of fruit!

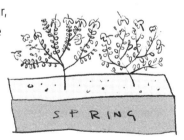

SUMMER

In the summer, the cranberry bogs become a hive of activity! Cranberry flowers have to be pollinated for them to turn into fruit, so farmers use bees to get the job done. Beekeepers bring beehives to the bogs (try saying that quickly!) and the bees get busy buzzing from flower to flower, collecting pollen and nectar as they go.

> BEEKEEPERS BRING BEEHIVES TO THE BOGS. BEEKEEPERS BRING BEEBIVES TO THE BOGS. BEEKEEPERS BING BEEBIVES TO THE BOBS.

Remember when we learned about pine seeds being pollinated in chapter two? Flip back to page 102 if you missed it. Well, another way that plants can become pollinated is when a bee drinks **nectar** (a sugary syrup) from a flower, and the dusty pollen brushes on to the bee's body. Then, when the bee visits another flower, the pollen brushes off on to the flower and pollinates it. This means the flower can turn into a fruit and the plant can make new seeds, so that more plants can grow in the future.

With plenty of sunshine and water, the cranberry flowers eventually drop their petals, and the fruit begins to grow. It doesn't look like a cranberry yet though – the fruit starts off a milky white colour and becomes ruby red as it gets older and ripens.

AUTUMN

By autumn, the cranberries are fully grown and ready to be harvested in time for Christmas. But how do you think farmers pick them? Well, it would be really fiddly to pick thousands of little cranberries by hand, so cranberry growers have come up with a clever plan that starts with flooding the bogs again!

FLOATING CRANBERRIES!

Cranberries have four air pockets inside them, and because of this, they float on water. (In fact, they'd make pretty good beachballs for beetles and armbands for chipmunks.) Famers use the floatiness of the cranberries to help them harvest the fruit.

To get all the cranberries off the vines, farmers use special machines called 'egg beaters'. They have this nickname because they help stir up the water, like you might beat some eggs to make a cake! Egg beaters look like metal trolleys with four massive wheels on the front, and farmers push them through the flooded bogs to make the wheels move round and round. This gets all the bog water sloshing about, which jiggles the fruit and knocks it off the vines. And because cranberries float, they all bob to the surface of the water, like hundreds of little buoys!

AND GIRLS!

Not boys. BUOYS.
The bright red round floating safety devices? Never mind.

And just like that, the bogs are transformed into bright-red, cranberry seas. Clever right?

Next, farmers use enormous rubber bands to drag the floating fruit into one corner of the bog. Here, a special tube sucks up all the cranberries and pumps them into the back of a truck that takes them to factories to be turned into juice and sauce. As soon as all the cranberries have been harvested, the water is drained from the bogs and the cycle is ready to begin again!

In some parts of North America and Canada, you can visit cranberry bogs in the autumn. The farmers let people paddle in the water and scoop up some floating cranberries to take home. How much fun does that sound? Would you like to splash around in a bog full of cranberries?

WHERE DO CHRISTMAS SPICES COME FROM?

As soon as Halloween is over, you might notice shops and cafes start selling Christmas-spiced drinks, Christmas-spiced cookies and Christmas-spiced candles. You can even get Christmas-spiced shower gel (I bet that's the one Father Christmas uses!).

But what makes the warm, spicy, Christmassy flavour that we find in mince pies, Christmas pudding and gingerbread? The key ingredients are **cinnamon**, **ginger**, **nutmeg** and **clove**. Mixing these spices together makes a delicious smell that reminds us of Christmas time!

WHAT IS A SPICE?

A **spice** is a dried part of a plant – such as its bark, roots, berries and seeds – that we use to make our food taste more exciting. The edible leaves of a plant are what we call **herbs**. Herbs can be used fresh or dry, but spices are always dried.

Spices started to become popular in England during the medieval times, when soldiers and sailors brought them back from far-flung corners of the world. At first, these exotic spices were very rare and expensive, so only rich people could afford them. Since Christmas was a time of big feasts, wealthy people started to use lots of spices in their traditional dishes. It made their food taste even more delicious, but it was also a way for people to show off how rich they were to their friends.

WHY DON'T MINCE PIES HAVE MINCE IN THEM?

You might have wondered why a sweet treat has mince in its name when it's nothing like the stuff you use to make spag Bol. Well, the original medieval version actually did have meat in it! It might sound gross, but it wasn't uncommon for medieval banquets to serve pies filled with both meat AND fruit, sugar and spices. This was partly because sugar helped preserve the meat, and partly as a way of showing that the host could afford fancy spices. Over the centuries, as sugar and spices became more easily available, we ditched the meat in mince pies – but the name lives on!

Let's find out about some of the most popular Christmas spices and discover where they come from . . .

CINNAMON

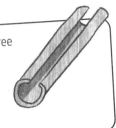

What plant does it come from? The cinnamon tree (*Cinnamomum verum*)
What part of the plant is it? Bark
Where does it come from? India, Sri Lanka, Bangladesh and Myanmar

Cinnamon is the dried bark of the cinnamon tree, which grows in countries such as Sri Lanka and India. To make cinnamon, you first have to slice and peel the bark off the tree. Next, you scrape away the rough bits until you're left with the soft and bendy inner bark. Then, you roll it up into little tubes called 'quills' or 'cinnamon sticks' and let them dry in the sun.

As the cinnamon bark dries, it turns a dark-brown colour and the flavour, which comes from the plant's natural oils, becomes much stronger. Cinnamon tastes sweet and woody, and it leaves your mouth feeling warm and tingly! Some people like to use whole cinnamon sticks in savoury dishes such as curries, and I love to use powdered cinnamon for baking puddings like apple pies.

But cinnamon isn't just tasty – it has some special properties too. Cinnamon oil can help stop bad bacteria and fungi from spreading, which is why people throughout history have used it to help fight off coughs and colds. The ancient Egyptians even used it for mummification. They would make a special mixture from cinnamon and rub it on the bodies of the dead before wrapping them up in linen strips to help stop them from rotting away. EEEWW! Sorry if I put you off your Christmas pudding!

CLOVES

What plant does it come from? Indonesian clove tree (*Syzygium aromaticum*)
What part of the plant is it? Flower bud
Where does it come from? Maluku Islands, Indonesia

Dried cloves look like small, reddish-brown, rusty nails. They even get their name from the Latin word '*clavus*', which means nail. But they don't always look like this, because cloves start life as beautiful red flower buds. The flowers grow in little clusters on the Indonesian clove tree. To make the spice, the flower buds have to be handpicked and dried before the petals have fully opened.

Cloves have a warm and fruity taste, but they also taste a bit like medicine. They are packed with a type of oil called 'eugenol', which gives them their medicinal flavour. Eugenol is a natural anaesthetic, which means it can have a numbing effect. If you were to chew on a whole clove you might find your tongue going a little numb, and your speech a little slurry. It's the reason why people have used cloves to treat toothache for hundreds of years!

❓ DID YOU KNOW ...

Cloves were also used as natural breath fresheners. Apparently, in 200 BCE (around 2,200 years ago) guests of the Chinese imperial court would hold a clove in their mouth so the emperor didn't have to deal with anyone's stinky breath!

GINGER

What plant does it come from? Ginger (*Zingiber*)
What part of the plant is it? Rhizome (underground stem)
Where does it come from? China, parts of Southeast Asia

Ginger is one of the most popular spices in the world. It is often mistaken as a root because it grows underground, but it is actually a type of **rhizome**. Rhizomes are thick, knobbly stems that grow just below the surface of the soil. They can send out shoots that grow up above the soil and roots that grow down, but their main job is to store sugar for the plant to use as energy during the cold winter months. The ginger rhizome looks a bit like a chubby, warty finger, with a pale-brown outer skin that can be peeled away to reveal a bright-yellow centre that has a citrusy smell.

The fresh, fiery ginger rhizome has been sliced and grated into Asian dishes like stir-fries and soups for thousands of years, but it's also used to bake Christmas goodies like gingerbread!

Ginger has also been used as a medicine for over 2,000 years. The ancient Chinese, Greeks and Romans all used it to fight off colds and help digestion, and pirates used it to calm seasickness.

Some cultures even believed that slapping ginger on someone's head would make their hair grow back.

QUICK! PASS ME THE GINGARRRRGHHHH!

This sounds pretty ridiculous, but actually the nutrients in ginger can nourish your hair, so it's not a totally random theory. Still, I wouldn't recommend grating the ingredients for tomorrow night's stir-fry on your head.

NUTMEG

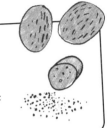

What plant does it come from? Fragrant nutmeg tree *(Myristica fragrans)*
What part of the plant is it? Seed (kernel)
Where does it come from? Banda Islands, part of the Maluku Islands archipelago, Indonesia

What part of a plant do you think nutmeg comes from? Surprisingly, it's not a nut!

This nutty lookalike is actually a seed that comes from the fruit of a nutmeg tree. Nutmeg fruit looks a little bit like a pear and in the middle is a stone that is wrapped in a bright-red, rubbery coating (I think it looks like strawberry laces!). When the stone is cracked open, it reveals a soft kernel. This is the seed we use as a spice. Once it's been removed from the stone, the nutmeg kernel is dried for about eight weeks and can be sold whole or ground up into a powder.

Nutmeg tastes sweet and nutty. During Christmas time, people sprinkle ground nutmeg on warm drinks, grate it into pies and mix it into creamy sauces. Long ago, nutmeg was so popular that people would carry a dried nutmeg kernel in a tiny silver box with a grater inside, so they could always grate a sprinkle of spice on to their food. These tiny personal graters were incredibly detailed, and some people even wore them as necklaces! They're still in use today.

Unfortunately, wealthy Europeans loved nutmeg so much that people were prepared to do just about anything to get hold of it.

Nutmeg trees originally grew on the beautiful islands of Banda in Indonesia, where they were looked after by the Bandanese people. But once European sailors discovered the spice, it became super popular, and in the 1600s a group of spice traders took over the islands. They forced the local Bandanese people to grow and hand over all their nutmeg, and those who refused to work for them were punished. The high price of nutmeg meant that the traders only cared about making money, no matter how harmful the farming was to the Bandanese people and their islands.

Sadly, these were not the only people who were harmed by ruthless spice traders. Many countries were treated badly and had their special local plants taken away from them. Nowadays, spices can be grown in other parts of the world, so there is more of them to go around. But it's important to remember the suffering caused by the spice trade, and know that wanting something doesn't mean that it is ours to take.

So now we know that spices have been used for thousands of years both to flavour food and cure illnesses, and that they were once so valuable that people were prepared to steal from others just to get their hands on them. It's a fascinating history, and a Christmas story that isn't often told. Maybe next time you enjoy a mince pie, you can think about where all those delicious spices have come from.

WHY DO WE BUILD GINGERBREAD HOUSES?

My favourite Christmas spice has to be ginger because I LOVE gingerbread. Not only is it delicious, it's also really strong! The right recipe will make a biscuit that's soft enough to cut when it's warm, and sturdy enough to build things with when it's cooled. The most famous gingerbread construction is, of course . . . the gingerbread house! But where do gingerbread houses come from?

The tradition of decorating gingerbread houses began in Germany in the 1800s. It's thought that the edible constructions became popular after the Brothers Grimm published their famous story, *Hansel and Gretel*. In this tale, two children find themselves lost in the woods and stumble upon a house made entirely of bread, cakes and sweets! It's every child's dream come true, but there's a catch – the house belongs to an evil witch who plans to eat the children. (Not very Christmassy, is it?!) Inspired by the story, German bakers began to create miniature versions of the witch's house out of *lebkuchen* – a type of spiced honey biscuit. These little houses were beautifully decorated with icing and other sweets, and they quickly became a popular holiday treat in Germany.

GINGERNEERING!

Here is one recipe that will help you design and engineer a gingerbread house so strong it could withstand a snowstorm. Aprons on – it's time to get gingerneering!

Gingerneering = Gingerbread + Engineering

P.S. Making gingerbread is super fun but it does take a long time, so it's totally cool if you pass on the baking and use ready-made gingerbread, square crackers or rectangular biscuits to gingerneer with instead.

You will need
For the gingerbread

- 250g unsalted butter
- 200g dark muscovado sugar
- 7 tbsp golden syrup
- 600g plain flour
- 2 tsp bicarbonate of soda
- 4 tsp ground ginger

The template

- a gingerbread house template (You can draw and measure out one of your own, or if you get really stuck, you can use one of the templates from one of the links on page 235)
- greaseproof or baking paper
- pencil
- scissors

The glue: royal icing

- 2 egg whites
- 500g icing sugar
- a piping bag

To decorate

- any sweet treats you like! You could use jelly sweets, candy canes, sprinkles, silver balls – the choice is yours!

Instructions

Make sure you ask permission from your Big Elf before you start gingerneering. You'll need them close by for all the cutting and baking!

1 Heat the oven to 200°C/180°C fan/gas mark 6.

2 Melt the butter, sugar and syrup in a pan.

3 Mix the flour, bicarbonate of soda and ground ginger in a large bowl, then stir in the melted butter mixture to make a stiff dough. If it won't quite come together, add a tiny splash of water.

4 Use a sheet of baking paper and a pencil to draw your template.

5 Cut out the template pieces, making sure to remember which is which!

6 Roll out the gingerbread dough on to another piece of baking paper to roughly the thickness of two £1 coins.

7 Place one of the template sections on to the rolled-out dough and cut round it.

8 Repeat with the remaining dough, re-rolling the trimmings, until you have two side walls, a front and back wall, and two roof panels.

9 Bake all the sections for 12 minutes (or until firm) and just a little darker at the edges. Leave to cool for a few minutes, then ask your Big Elf to trim around the templates again to give clean, sharp edges. Leave to cool completely.

10 To make the royal icing, put the egg whites in a large bowl, sift in the icing sugar and then stir to make a thick, smooth icing. Spoon the icing into a piping bag.

11 Pipe the icing along the wall edges and join the walls together. Use a small bowl to support the walls from the inside, and allow the icing to dry.

12 Once the icing is completely dry, remove the supports and attach the roof panels to the walls with some more icing.

13 Sit tight and wait for the icing to dry before you start decorating.

14 Use the leftover icing to glue on your chosen sweet treats!

TA-DA! You have gingerneered a delicious gingerbread house!

BONUS GINGERNEERING

Measuring out ingredients, creating a template, planning your construction and being creative are all the kind of STEM skills needed by engineers, architects and gingerneers alike! To put these skills to the test, you could try:

- **Experimenting with different types of glue for your gingerbread house – how about melted marshmallows?**

- **Testing the strength of your gingerbread house – does it fall down if you roll a marble into the walls?**

- **Building a gingerbread train or even a gingerbread bridge!**

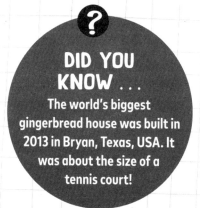

?

DID YOU KNOW . . .

The world's biggest gingerbread house was built in 2013 in Bryan, Texas, USA. It was about the size of a tennis court!

HOW ARE CANDY CANES MADE?

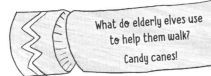

What do elderly elves use to help them walk?

Candy canes!

As well as making excellent walking sticks for elves, candy canes are a yummy, minty treat and a great way to liven up your Christmas tree. But who invented the candy cane?

The answer is . . . well, we don't really know the answer to this one. There's one legend that says a German choirmaster handed out candy sticks to children at a Christmas Nativity service so they would have something to suck on to keep them quiet. The choirmaster came up with the idea to bend the sticks into the shape of a cane to represent a shepherd's staff, just like the ones in the Nativity Story!

This is a brilliant story but it's hard to know if it's completely true. It's also possible that **confectioners** simply added the hook to sugar sticks to make them easier to hang on Christmas trees.

A confectioner is someone who makes and sells sweets.

Today, most candy canes are made in factories by machines, but there are still some people who make them by hand. It's a bit like doing one big science experiment! Let's find out how candy canes are made and get stuck into some sweet sugar science . . .

DISSOLVING

To make candy canes you need three main ingredients:

- **white sugar**
- **a thick, gloopy sugar called glucose (or corn syrup)**
- **water**

All three ingredients are put in a massive pan and heated to a very high temperature. As the sugar, glucose and water are heated together, the sugar **dissolves**. This means that the sugar breaks down and spreads evenly throughout the water until it looks like it has disappeared. The clear, sweet liquid is called a **sugar solution**.

EVAPORATING

When the sugar solution starts to boil, the super-high temperature causes the water to **evaporate**. This is when water heats up so much it turns from liquid into a gas and rises out of the pan. With less water in the solution, the mixture transforms into thick, sticky syrup.

CRYSTALLIZING

When the temperature and the amount of water and sugar in the solution are just right, the sugar molecules will begin to attract each other and arrange themselves into solid crystals. This process is called **crystallization**, and it's what makes candy canes solid. It's a bit like a pile of loose building blocks coming together and stacking themselves into a sturdy shape. As the sugar syrup cools, more and more sugar molecules come together to form larger crystals, which makes the candy start to harden.

COOLING

When the sugar syrup has reached the right temperature, it's poured on to a special table made of **granite**. Granite is a type of stone that feels cool to the touch. This makes it a great material to help gently cool down the hot syrup.

To make the candy canes colourful and tasty, the confectioner separates the syrup into different piles and adds a few drops of flavouring and colouring. Peppermint with red and white stripes tends to be the most common combination, but candy canes can be made in any flavour or colour that you like!

WHAT ABOUT SARDINE FLAVOUR?

OK, maybe not ANY flavour . . .

After the syrup has cooled down a little, it will have a thick, sticky texture (a bit like slime!) and it begins to look more like candy.

PULLING

Next, the confectioner will start a process called 'pulling', which involves stretching and folding the candy over and over again like plasticine. This traps little bubbles of air between the sugar. Without the extra air bubbles, the candy would be too hard to crunch and could crack your teeth. Ouch!

SHAPING

After the candy is pulled, it's time to shape it into candy canes!

- **The confectioner takes a big chunk of pulled white candy and a smaller chunk of pulled red candy and rolls them into long sausages.**

- **Then, the red sausage and the white sausage are twisted together to make a rope shape, creating a cool spiral pattern that gives the candy cane its stripes!**

- **The red-and-white rope is then cut into short sticks and one end of each stick is bent over to make it look like a cane.**

- **Finally, the candy canes are left to cool and harden so that we can enjoy them as a sweet treat or hang them on the Christmas tree!**

?

DID YOU KNOW . . .

Around 1.76 BILLION candy canes are sold every year. If you lined them all up, those candy canes would stretch approximately 140,000 miles – that's enough candy canes to go around the world five-and-a-half times!

SANTA'S MAGIC MILK!

Do you leave a mince pie and a glass of milk for Father Christmas on Christmas Eve? If you do, I have an experiment that is a brilliant science magic trick to impress your friends and family with – give it a try and pour the leftover milk into a glass for Father Christmas!

You will need

- whole milk
- a plate or a shallow dish
- red and green food colourings
- a cotton bud, lolly stick or a small strip of cardboard
- washing-up liquid

Optional Christmassy extras

- edible glitter
- peppermint essence

Make sure you ask permission from your Big Elf before you try this magic science trick!

1. Pour some milk on to the plate. If you want to make this experiment extra festive, then you could add a few drops of peppermint essence to the milk.

2. Sprinkle some glitter on top of the milk if you like, and squeeze a few drops of red and green food colouring in the centre of the dish.

3. Place the end of a cotton bud into the centre of the milk. Notice how nothing happens?

4. Now, squeeze a tiny amount of washing-up liquid on to the cotton bud.

5. Place the soapy cotton bud in the centre of the milk and watch the Christmas magic in action!

THE SCIENCE BIT – WHY DOES THE SOAP MAKE THE FOOD COLOURING AND GLITTER SWIRL?

To understand what is happening in this experiment, it's important to know that milk is mostly made of water. Water is made of molecules that cling on to each other. At the water's surface, they cling on even tighter – a bit like they're holding hands. *Awww!* This hand-holding makes a thin layer on the top of the water that we call **surface tension**.

Because milk is made of lots of water, the rules of surface tension work the same for a dish of milk too. Milk also contains vitamins, minerals and, importantly, fats. And there is something we use in this experiment that loves fats but doesn't like water – soap!

One end of a soap molecule LOVES water, and scientists describe this as **hydrophilic**. However, the other side HATES water but loves oil and fat, which is described as **hydrophobic** (think of it as like having a 'phobia' of water!). Soap is great for cleaning greasy dishes because the hydrophobic ends pick up greasy fats, while the hydrophilic ends join with the water molecules and get washed away, taking all the oily, dirty stuff away with them.

When we add a drop of soap to the milk, the soap molecules break the surface tension of the liquid. The hydrophobic ends of the soap molecules go chasing after the fat molecules in the milk, and the hydrophilic ends of the soap want to cling on to the water molecules. As the molecules chase each other around the dish, the food colouring and glitter that settled on top of the mixture get whizzed around too! And that's what creates the magical milky illusion.

If you're not too full after all that Christmas feasting, maybe you've got a little room for something else? How about a CHINESE NEW YEAR'S EVE feast!

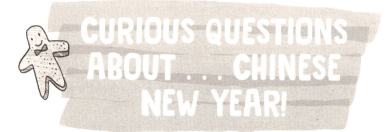

CURIOUS QUESTIONS ABOUT . . . CHINESE NEW YEAR!

Chinese New Year is one of the most important holidays for Chinese people round the world, and food is a huge part of it. Chinese New Year's Eve typically involves a massive banquet with enough food for plenty of leftovers on New Year's Day. To find out more about this delicious celebration, I spoke to ten-year-old Isabella, who lives with her mummy, Adia, her daddy and her twin sisters, Amelia and Alice. First, I asked Isabella and Adia to explain why Chinese New Year is so important to their family . . .

ISABELLA

ADIA

ISABELLA, CAN YOU TELL ME WHAT CHINESE NEW YEAR IS ALL ABOUT?

IT'S ABOUT CELEBRATING THE NEW YEAR AND TRYING TO GATHER GOOD LUCK AS YOU WASH AWAY ALL THE BAD LUCK BEFORE THE NEW YEAR STARTS.

AND IS THERE ANYTHING UNIQUE ABOUT HOW YOUR FAMILY CELEBRATES CHINESE NEW YEAR?

MY FAMILY IS HALF MALAYSIAN, SO THEY FOLLOW SOME MALAYSIAN TRADITIONS. BUT MY PARENTS CAME TO ENGLAND AND RAISED ME HERE, AND THIS IS ALSO WHERE ISABELLA HAS GROWN UP. SO, WE'VE CHOSEN ALL OUR FAVOURITE TRADITIONS AND DISHES FROM DIFFERENT CHINESE CULTURES AND MIXED THEM TOGETHER!

WHEN IS CHINESE NEW YEAR?

Chinese New Year is a fifteen-day festival that marks the beginning of the new year according to the Chinese lunar calendar, which follows the movements of the Moon and the Sun. Every month starts with a new moon, which is when the Moon looks completely dark when viewed from Earth. The new year starts on the new moon that falls between the winter solstice (the shortest day of the year) and the spring equinox (the first day of spring). So, the dates can change, but it's always sometime between 21 January and 20 February.

WHAT IS THE CHINESE ZODIAC?

Each year of the Chinese lunar calendar is represented by an animal called a zodiac sign. There are twelve animals in the Chinese zodiac:

RAT
OX
TIGER
RABBIT
DRAGON
SNAKE
HORSE
GOAT
MONKEY
ROOSTER
DOG
PIG

There are many different stories for how the zodiac animals were chosen, but one version says that a great Chinese ruler known as the Jade Emperor held a race for all the animals in his kingdom.

The twelve animals who took part would each have a year named after them, and whatever position they came in the race would decide the order of the animals. Every animal had to cross a large river to reach the finish line. The race was full of twists and turns – from the rat who hitched a ride on the ox's head to come in first place, to the pig who stopped for a snack, fell asleep and finished last!

Sorry you two – there aren't any penguins or yetis in the Chinese zodiac. You might have noticed there isn't a cat in the story either. One version says that the cat was invited to the race, but their sneaky neighbour, the rat, deliberately didn't wake them up on the day. So cats and rats have been said to be enemies from then on!

WHAT WAS THE ZODIAC ANIMAL FOR THE YEAR YOU WERE BORN?

YEAR OF THE DRAGON.

SAME! WE'RE BOTH DRAGONS. NICE!

It's said that people have certain personality traits based on their zodiac animal. Isabella and I were both born in years of the dragon, which suggests we are confident and lucky! Do you know what your zodiac sign is?

HOW DO FAMILIES PREPARE FOR CHINESE NEW YEAR?

That sounds like a great way to start the new year! Some people even believe that it's best not to clean for a few days after Chinese New Year, so as not to sweep away the good luck.

DO PEOPLE GIVE GIFTS FOR CHINESE NEW YEAR?

Instead of presents, children are traditionally given red packets or envelopes for Chinese New Year.

WHAT'S A RED PACKET?

SO, THEY'RE THE COLOUR RED TO WARD OFF BAD SPIRITS AND THEY'RE FILLED WITH MONEY.

Red is considered a lucky colour in Chinese culture, so giving a red envelope to friends and family is a way of passing on good luck and protecting them against evil for the year ahead.

WHY IS FOOD SO IMPORTANT TO CHINESE NEW YEAR?

ISABELLA, WHAT DOES YOUR CHINESE NEW YEAR'S EVE FEAST INVOLVE?

WE HAVE EIGHT OR NINE DIFFERENT DISHES, WHICH ALL HAVE THEIR OWN SPECIAL MEANING!

In Chinese culture, objects and foods can symbolize good or bad luck if they *sound* like other words with good or bad meanings. And because Chinese New Year is all about bringing good luck into the coming year, it's celebrated with lots of different foods that have lucky meanings.

For example, the Chinese numbers eight and nine sound like the words for 'prosperity' (which means wealth and success) and 'a long time' – so having eight or nine dishes on Chinese New Year's Eve is thought to bring prosperity for a long time to come!

To help us understand more about the dishes and their meanings, Isabella and her mum, Adia, have drawn us a menu of their traditional Chinese New Year's Eve celebratory feast!

ISABELLA'S CHINESE NEW YEAR'S EVE MENU

1. Steamed fish with ginger and onions (often grouper or sea bass)
In Simplified Chinese, the word for fish sounds like the word 'abundance', which means having more than you need of something.

2. Fried fish with ginger and onions
This fried dish isn't for Chinese New Year's Eve. It's made using the leftover steamed fish so it can be eaten on New Year's Day.

3. Boiled prawns with garlic soy dip
The word for prawn in Cantonese sounds like '*ha*', which symbolizes laughter for the new year.

4. Stewed dried oysters, pork, mushroom and black moss
This dish is symbolic of wishing someone 'good things and wealth' for the new year.

5. Steamed chicken with ginger-and-spring-onion sauce
The whole chicken in this dish symbolizes . . . wholeness!

6. Lion's head meatballs – pork meatballs with sticky sauce and vegetables
Some people think these large meatballs look like a lion's head with a 'mane' of leafy vegetables around them! Lions are symbolic of strength, and the round meatballs symbolize family unity.

7. Longevity noodles
Long noodles are considered to be a lucky food, as the length of the noodles represents long life and happiness.

8. Sweet rice balls
These are made of rice flour and sometimes have sweet fillings such as red bean or sesame paste. The round balls symbolize togetherness and reunion.

MADDIE'S CURIOUS CHRISTMAS QUIZ – ROUND THREE

Phew, that was a lot of tasty Christmas food. I hope you're not too stuffed to tackle some tough questions!

1. What was the most popular dish placed in the centre of a royal medieval banquet?

2. Which country do turkeys come from originally?

3. Which fast food do people eat on Christmas Day in Japan?

4. Where do some European people keep their Christmas carp before they cook it?

5. What chemical makes Brussels sprouts smell like rotten eggs?

6. What type of wetland habitat do cranberries grow in?

7. Where do mince pies get their name?

8. What part of a plant is a clove?

9. What classic fairy tale made gingerbread houses popular?

10. What is it called when confectioners stretch and fold sugar?

Answers on page 233

FUN AND DECORATIONS

Right, now that dinner is over, it's time for the entertainment part of the evening. This chapter is all about FESTIVE FUN STUFF – I'm talking glittery decorations, flying panto fairies, speeding sledges and oodles of wrapping paper. So let's kick it off with a bang, shall we?

BANG!

ARGHH! NOT YET, NIGEL.

Ahem. Where was I? Oh yes . . .

WHY DO CRACKERS GO BANG?

Christmas crackers are a British tradition so beloved that many of us couldn't imagine Christmas dinner without one. But for anyone unfamiliar with the Christmas cracker, let me take you through this EXPLOSIVE ritual.

Once everyone has taken their seats at the table – in our house this normally involves a bit of a kerfuffle as we fetch the 'emergency chairs' from the shed – the first thing we pick up is a cracker. It's a cardboard tube, wrapped in brightly coloured paper and twisted at both ends. We rattle it close to our ears as we try to guess what tiny treasure might be hiding inside. Then, we all cross our arms and each grab the end of someone else's cracker, making a (slightly chaotic) chain, and the countdown can begin . . .

ONE . . .

TWO . . .

On 'THREE!' everyone pulls, the crackers rip apart and a loud **BANG** fills the air!

Finally, everyone squeals in delight as they hurry to find the cracker's contents, which have normally spilled all over the table and floor. Traditionally, whoever ends up with the bigger part of the cracker wins the contents, but in our house we share it all out, so everyone ends up with a paper crown, a silly joke and a small gift – it might be a tiny plastic leapfrog, a fortune-telling fish or the ever-popular multipack of miniature screwdrivers. (Grown-ups genuinely love these because they're small enough to fix their reading glasses!)

Pulling crackers is a brilliant way to get everyone in the festive spirit, but why do we have tiny explosives on our Christmas table in the first place? Surely that's a bit dangerous?

Well, it all started in the Victorian times when Tom Smith, a London-based sweet shop owner, travelled to Paris in search of inspiration. Ooh, la la.

Here, Tom discovered the French 'bon bon' – a sugared almond wrapped in a twist of tissue paper. He quickly started selling them in his London shop, and the sweets soon became a popular Christmas treat. To encourage his customers to buy more, Tom added a little love message inside the paper to make each one unique.

Then one day, the story goes, Tom was sitting by a fire listening to the crackling logs and had a brilliant idea that would make his sweets truly unforgettable. He bought some tiny explosive 'snaps' from a fireworks company and hid them inside his sweet wrappers. He renamed the sweets 'Bangs of Expectation', and the first Christmas cracker was born!

Tom Smith's cracker business was a huge success. His company even made special crackers for the royal family!

Over the years, the almond was replaced with a small gift, the paper crown was added, and the mushy love poems were swapped for corny jokes. Talking of which . . .

What do you get if you cross Father Christmas with a duck?

A Christmas quacker!

It's easy to understand why people love crackers so much. Who doesn't love a silly present and a loud noise that makes people laugh? But where does this noise actually come from?

HOW DO CRACKERS WORK?

Crackers contain a tiny patch of an explosive chemical called silver fulminate, which has a reputation for being EXTREMELY sensitive. Now I don't mean it bursts into tears at soppy films or has a strop when it doesn't get its sardines (I'm looking at you, Puddles). I mean that it explodes *really* easily. If you had enough of it in a pile, just the weight of a falling feather on it could make the whole lot go KABOOM! Silver fulminate's sensitive, explosive nature makes it dangerous in large quantities, but it's perfectly safe to use in small amounts inside Christmas crackers.

If you carefully open a cracker, you will find a cracker snap inside. It's made of two long, thin strips of card that are attached end to end with a slight overlap.

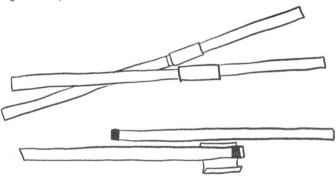

Beneath the overlap are two materials: a tiny patch of white powder (this is the silver fulminate) and a rough piece of material that feels a bit like sandpaper. When the cracker is pulled from both ends, the **friction** between these two materials creates a small explosion, and we hear that famous cracker bang.

WHAT IS FRICTION?

Friction is a force that slows or stops the movement of two surfaces that are sliding over each other. If you rub your hands together in opposite directions, you'll be able to feel friction. Go on, pop the book down and give it a go for a few seconds! Did you notice your hands getting warm? That's because the surface of your hands is not completely flat and smooth, so it takes energy to slide them across each other, and some of that energy becomes heat.

The amount of friction depends on the materials from which the two surfaces are made – the rougher the surface, the more friction is produced. The material inside the cracker snap is very rough and the silver fulminate is super sensitive. So when we pull a cracker apart and force the strips of cardboard to slide over each other, the friction between the two materials produces heat, and this makes the silver fulminate go . . .

So now you know why we have crackers and what makes them go BANG! Just remember that while crackers are safe and lots of fun when we use them properly, they shouldn't be played with or opened up unless a Big Elf is on hand to help.

HOW DO NUTCRACKERS WORK?

Now we're going to look at a different kind of cracker – a NUTcracker!

Have you ever seen a nutcracker at Christmas time? They often look like little wooden soldiers in a smart red uniform. You might have noticed these festive characters have big, chomping teeth. Well, as the name suggests, those teeth are for cracking nuts! Traditional nutcrackers have a handle at the back that opens their mouth so a nut can be placed inside, and when the handle is pressed down the teeth snap together and break the nut open.

A CRACKING STORY

Humans have been using tools to crack nuts for MILLIONS of years, with early humans using rocks to smash open tough shells. We aren't the only species to work this out either. Primates such as chimpanzees, long-tailed macaques and bearded capuchin monkeys have all been seen using heavy stones to crack nuts open!

It wasn't until nineteenth-century Germany when sophisticated wooden nutcrackers carved into the shape of soldiers, known as 'nussknackers', would became popular. However, it was in 1892, when the composer Tchaikovsky set his famous ballet *The Nutcracker* on Christmas Eve, that these cracking toys became a symbol of Christmas!

Today, most nutcrackers that you see at Christmas time are purely for decoration, but some people (including me) still enjoy cracking open a nutty treat after their dinner.

YUCK! WE WANT DOUGHNUTS!

(SIGH) YOU TWO ARE TOUGH NUTS TO CRACK . . .

?

DID YOU KNOW . . .

The world's largest working nutcracker can be found in Germany at the Erstes Nussknacker Museum. It is just over 10 metres tall – that's about the same height as two giraffes stacked on top of each other – and can even crack coconuts!

Nutcrackers come in all shapes and sizes, but they are all examples of **simple machines**. A basic nutcracker that you might find in your kitchen is made of two metal bars attached with a **hinge**.

A hinge is a piece of metal that joins two parts together and allows them to open and close.

To crack a nut – or do other types of work – we need a certain amount of **force**. But there is a limit to how much force our bodies can create, so we can use simple machines to help us. They make certain jobs easier by increasing the effect of the force we put into the work.

A force is a push or pull on an object.

A nutcracker uses a simple machine called a **lever** to produce the force needed to crack the shell. A basic lever looks like a long bar balanced on something called a **fulcrum**. When we push down on one end of the lever, the fulcrum makes the other end go up – just like a seesaw at the playground! Levers can help us lift things that are too heavy for us to lift on our own. In a seesaw, the fulcrum is in the middle, between the **effort** (the place where the force is being applied) and the **load** (the thing that you are trying to put force on). All levers connect these same three parts: the fulcrum, the effort and the load.

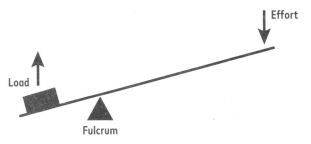

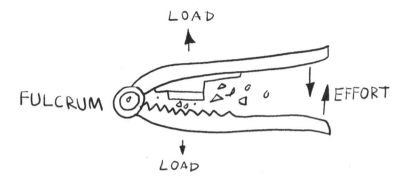

LOAD

FULCRUM

EFFORT

LOAD

The difference between a seesaw and a nutcracker is that the fulcrum and the load are in different places. The nutcracker's fulcrum is the point where the two bars are joined together. The effort (the place we push down) is applied at the other end of the fulcrum and the load (the nut to be cracked open) lies in the middle. When we apply effort and squeeze the bars at one end, the fulcrum increases the effect of that force on the nut in the middle, and this helps us crack the shell and get to the tasty kernel on the inside.

CRACK!

Of course, if you don't have a nutcracker, you can always hire the help of a friendly abominable snowman to smash up your shells. Or ask a Big Elf to use a hammer. Either will work.

After all that nutcracking, I think we should shell-ebrate with a snack! Walnut, anyone?

WALNUT-SHELL REINDEER!

Once you've cracked a whole load of walnuts and eaten the delicious kernels, you're left with a pile of shells. Rather than throw them away, what could you make with them?

A HELMET FOR BIRDS?

A SNAIL COSTUME FOR SLUGS?

SOME CLOGS FOR A SQUIRREL?

HOW ABOUT A CHRISTMAS DECORATION?

You will need

- a black pen (or googly eyes)
- brown felt (or brown paper/card)
- a knife
- PVA glue
- a walnut shell (split into two halves)
- ribbon (or string)
- a red mini pompom (felt or card or a button would also work)

Instructions

It is very important to ask a Big Elf to split your walnuts in half. This can be done with a nutcracker (although this takes some careful walnut placement and a bit of luck!), or by placing the tip of a knife into the 'hinge' of a walnut shell and giving it a push and twist. Please be careful when using knives because they can be very sharp!

1. Draw two little antlers on the brown felt, then carefully cut them out (with the help of a Big Elf!).

2. Apply a generous amount of glue round the edge of one walnut-shell half.

3. Position the two antlers on either side of the narrow part of the glued walnut shell and place a loop of ribbon between them.

4. Carefully press the two halves together, sandwiching the antlers and ribbon.

5. Use your finger to wipe away any excess glue, then hold tight while it dries.

6. When the glue is dry, use a blob of glue to stick the red pompom on the tip of the walnut for the reindeer's nose, and use the pen to draw on two black, beady eyes (or stick on your googly eyes).

7. Your walnut-shell reindeer is finished! Perhaps you could hang it on a tree with some more walnut reindeer to make a whole herd?

HOW DO FAIRY LIGHTS WORK?

You'll know by now that I LOVE Christmas decorations – especially homemade ones – and fairy lights can add the perfect finishing touch. They bring a magical twinkle to dark spaces on winter evenings. BUT fairy lights can also be a right pain in the bum . . .

When I was younger, I would help my dad to carefully put away the fairy lights, winding them around a piece of cardboard to stop them getting tangled before they went back in the box marked 'XMAS DECS' in the loft. But no matter how careful we had been, next December would come round and the moment we plugged them back in, not a single pesky light bulb would work!

The only way to fix the lights was to spend HOURS testing each and every bulb to figure out which one was broken so that we could get the whole set shining again. But why does one broken bulb stop all the others from working? Let's find out!

Fairy lights are a long string of miniature light bulbs that are connected by wire in a big loop. To make them light up, they have to be powered by a source of **electricity**, such as a battery pack or an electricity socket. For electricity to get to all the light bulbs on the loop, it has to flow through the wire along a specific path, and we call this path a **circuit**!

The word 'circuit' sounds like a type of shape. What shape do you think that is?

Just like a circle, a circuit goes round and round without any spaces or gaps in it. If we make a gap in the path, the flow of electricity will stop, and it won't be able to get from the source of electricity to all of the light bulbs.

There are two main types of electrical circuit that fairy lights can be arranged in: **series** and **parallel**. They work in slightly different ways and which one they use will determine how easy it is to fix a set of broken lights!

Electricity is fascinating but it can be dangerous, so you should never handle fairy lights without a Big Elf.

SERIES

When we arrange fairy lights in **series**, it means they are all connected by a single wire. The little bulbs are connected one after the other, with the last wire completing the circuit to form a single loop. This means there is only one path for the electricity to flow along.

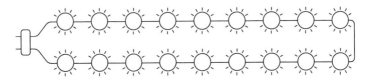

In a series circuit, if one bulb breaks, the path becomes blocked, and all the other lights stop working. The electricity stops flowing in the circuit because the broken bulb makes a gap in the pathway, so the electricity cannot flow all the way round. The only way to fix fairy lights that are arranged in series is to test every single light to find the broken bulb, and then replace it. This will close the gap in the circuit, complete the pathway and electricity will be able to flow once again.

This is why it took my dad hours and hours to fix the fairy lights when I was younger. He had to check every single bulb one by one until he found the broken one. But luckily there is a slightly more reliable way to arrange fairy lights – using a **parallel circuit**.

PARALLEL

When we arrange fairly lights in **parallel**, the bulbs are connected on different branches of the circuit. You can normally tell if your fairy lights are arranged in parallel because there will be two wires connecting each bulb. This means there are multiple paths for the electricity to flow along. In a parallel circuit, if a bulb breaks or becomes disconnected, the other lights can continue to shine. This is because the electricity can still flow along the remaining unbroken pathways!

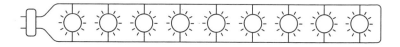

Most modern fairy lights are arranged in parallel, so fixing broken lights is much quicker than it used to be. So just in case your family is on the hunt for new lights, remind your Big Elf to look for fairy lights that are connected by two wires – it might save them a lot of time in the future!

So now you know how fairy lights work, but perhaps you're wondering where their name comes from? Because as we've just learned, fairy lights are powered by electricity and NOT fairy magic (boring, I know). But the real reason is still pretty cool . . .

In 1881, the Savoy (a swanky London hotel) became the first public building in the whole world to have electricity! A clever inventor named Sir Joseph Swan made 1,200 light bulbs to light up the whole place. A year later, the owner of the Savoy's theatre asked Sir Joseph to make smaller lights to decorate the fairy dresses of the performers in an opera. The lights were powered by little battery packs hidden in the costumes, making the actors glow just like real fairies! Audiences loved the little fairy lights so much that soon wealthy ladies started wearing them as fashion accessories (sounds like glowing off if you ask me . . .). Meanwhile, in America, a man called Edward Johnson became the first person to hang a string of electric lights on a Christmas tree, and the festive fairy light tradition was born.

Talking of theatre, fairies and costumes, it's time to head to a theatre to watch a pantomime!

WHAT IS PANTOMIME?

Have you ever been to a pantomime? What was that?
OH NO, you haven't? (Sorry, I'll stop the panto jokes now.)

In case you actually haven't seen one, a pantomime is a traditional musical play that lots of British families go to every year at Christmas. 'Panto' is often based on fairy tales and traditional stories, such as *Snow White and the Seven Dwarves*, *Jack and the Beanstalk*, *Cinderella* and *Peter Pan*. But no matter the story, certain things happen in every single pantomime that audiences always look forward to.

- Songs and dance routines.

ALWAYS LOOK ON THE BRIGHT SIDE OF LIFE . . .

- Silly jokes and slapstick comedy where the actors pretend to get hurt or are covered in a sloppy mess, like falling over and getting hundreds of custard pies in the face!

- Classic characters such as the hero, the villain and the dame – a funny male actor dressed up to play an older woman who will have lots of different extravagant costume changes and silly lines to say.

- LOTS of audience interaction. The audience is encouraged to cheer the goodies, boo the baddies, and shout responses to classic pantomime lines.

OH NO, THEY DONT!

OH YES, THEY DO!

- **Illusions and transformations in which things move or change on stage as if by magic! These include things like Cinderella's dress changing from rags to riches, Jack climbing an enormous beanstalk to the land of giants or Aladdin riding a flying carpet.**

You might think pantomime is just a silly bit of fun, but it has an amazing history and comes from a long theatrical tradition. Panto was originally inspired by an Italian theatre style called *commedia dell'arte*, which used dance, music, slapstick comedy and a cast of mischievous characters. The hilarious *commedia* characters were very popular and soon made their way on to London stages, and these English comedy plays became the early versions of panto.

It wasn't till the Victorian times that speech, jokes, puns and audience participation all became part of the show. Over the years, the productions became more and more over-the-top, with some London pantomimes lasting up to five hours! They featured stunning costumes, huge casts and special effects. Trapdoors, mirrors and flying systems were used to create magical illusions, such as flying a fairy on to the stage.

But how does a pantomime fairy fly?

Of course! But we also need the help of SCIENCE!

HOW DO PANTOMIME FAIRIES FLY?

Let me set you a scene.

It's the opening night of *The All-New Adventures of Peter Pan* and I'm standing nervously backstage, waiting to make my first-ever appearance as the famous mischievous fairy, Tinkerbell. Underneath my sparkly green dress, I'm wearing a **harness** – a kind of super seat belt that's wrapped round my legs and hips. Someone backstage takes two strong metal wires and clips them on to the harness through the secret holes in my dress. They whisper, 'Are you ready?' I'm not sure if I am. My heart is beating incredibly fast and I'm worried I might forget my lines. But I think happy thoughts and tell them, 'Yes'.

Suddenly, the wires start to move, and I'm lifted off the ground and hanging in mid-air! I dangle off-stage for a few seconds that feel like hours, and as soon as the music starts to play, the wires move again and I'm flown on to the stage to see 750 pairs of eyes staring back at me.

That was my first time flying as a pantomime fairy, and boy was it nerve-racking! But now I get to share with you how the magic really works behind the scenes.

To make a pantomime fairy fly, we need to use another simple machine. Only this time, instead of a lever, we're going to use something called a **pulley**. Pulleys are often used to help us lift heavy things. If a person tried to lift me above their head while I sang, danced and waved my wand about, they would get tired VERY quickly, but a pulley makes the job much easier.

Pulleys are all around us. We use them to open and close window blinds, go up and down elevators, raise sails on sailboats and lift construction materials with cranes. There are lots of types of pulleys, but for this explanation, we're going to focus on a simple pulley system that could lift a person and make them fly in a theatre.

To help, I will be playing the part of the flying pantomime fairy, and Nigel and Puddles will be the **stage technicians** – the people who work backstage to make all the sound, lights and special effects work.

Pulleys have two main parts: a wheel and some kind of rope or wire. The wheel on the pulley is special because it has a groove (a long, narrow dip) that goes all the way round it. The rope fits inside this groove so it can slide over the wheel without slipping out of place. The thing that is being lifted (that's me, the fairy!) is called the load and this has to be attached to the pulley. When the rope is pulled, the load goes up!

Let's break the flying pulley system down step by step.

First, Nigel and Puddles attach the pulley and a long rope to something called a **fly bar**. This is a long bar that runs high above the stage and can be moved up and down so theatre technicians can attach things like scenery and pulleys to it.

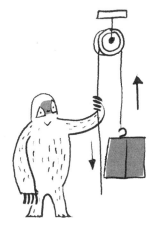

Next, one end of the rope is attached to a loop on my secret harness using a strong metal clip called a **carabiner**. The harness will hold me safely in the air but seeing it kind of ruins the magical illusion. So costume designers cleverly hide them under clothes and make gaps in the costumes for the ropes to run through.

Finally, when I'm safely clipped on to the rope, it's time to lift me up. When Nigel and Puddles apply some force by pulling down on the rope, the wheel on the fly bar turns and I'll go up into the air!

WOOHOO!

I went up, but that was still pretty difficult for our stage technicians! A single pulley changes the direction of the force. The means it allows the technicians to pull *down* to lift me *up*. However, the amount of effort Nigel and Puddles have to put in to do the work doesn't change, so to give them an advantage and make sure they don't have to put in as much effort, we have to introduce a second pulley.

Using two pulleys means you only need half the force to lift the load, which means you don't need to put in as much effort. A system with two or more pulleys is called a **block and tackle** and is often used to lift large, difficult-shaped objects, such as people. Adding more wheels to the block and tackle increases the load it can lift.

Let's try again . . .

ONE. TWO. THREE. PULL!

WEEEEE! I'M SO HIGH!

It worked! And this time, Puddles and Nigel didn't even break a sweat (which is lucky, because yeti sweat smells pretty gross . . .)

HOW DO YOU MAKE A TOBOGGAN GO FASTER?

After all that time in the air, I think we should come back down to Earth and try one of Puddles's favourite activities: tobogganing!

You might be thinking, *Hang on, I've never seen a penguin on a toboggan.* But maybe you've seen a video of a penguin sliding along the ice on their belly? Well, this behaviour is actually called *tobogganing*, only penguins do it just with their bodies!

Penguins are pretty slow walkers because they can only waddle on their little legs. But if they toboggan, they can move faster without worrying about falling over. On flat ice, Puddles lies down on her front, slides and pushes herself along using her feet and flippers. But on a downward slope . . . watch out! She's like a tiny black-and-white torpedo zooming down those hills at top speeds!

What's black and white,
black and white, black and white?
A penguin rolling down a hill!

People (and yetis) can't slide as well as penguins because our bodies aren't as smooth (sorry, Nigel). Instead, we have to use a wooden or plastic toboggan – but we still might struggle to catch a speeding penguin – especially if the toboggan keeps getting stuck in the snow.

What do you think we can do to make our toboggan go faster? There are a couple of things we can try, using our knowledge of forces:

- **Pushing off hard at the top of the slope will create more speed, giving us more momentum. Momentum is the force or speed of a moving object. The more momentum an object has, the faster it will travel.**
- **Adding lots of weight to the toboggan will also help us to go faster and travel further. Heavier objects have more momentum, which makes them harder to stop.**

But, hang on – Nigel and I have tried both these things. Why are we still getting stuck? It's because the fluffy snow is bunching up and pushing back on the moving toboggan, creating friction that slows it down. We know that smooth surfaces will have less friction than rough ones, so how can we make our toboggan ride smoother?

- **Swapping a rough wooden toboggan for a plastic one will reduce friction, so the toboggan will go faster.**
- **Smoothing the powdery snow into a slippery track will allow the toboggan to slide more easily over the snow and create even less friction.**

Right, we've grabbed a plastic toboggan and Puddles is going to slide down first on her belly to make a smooth toboggan run. Is there anything else we need?

A steeper slope!

- **On a steep hill, gravity pulls you down more strongly than on a gentle slope. This makes your momentum increase and you speed up more quickly.**

OK, we've found the perfect slope, a speedy toboggan and a slippery smooth track, Let's go!

THREE, TWO, ONE, PUSH!

WEEEEEEEE!!!!!

You could say that was a big peng-WIN! Our toboggan went much faster, and it's all thanks to using our knowledge of forces.

TABLETOP
ICE-HOCKEY RINK!

You might not have enough snow at Christmas to go tobogganing, but here's how you can try a winter sport in the comfort of your own home! This tabletop ice-hockey rink is perfect for all year round (although I'm afraid you're unlikely to make the team for the Winter Olympics with this particular sport . . .)

You will need

- scissors
- a piece of white paper, large enough to fit inside the tray
- an aluminium foil tray
- PVA glue
- a red and a blue crayon
- water
- two pipe cleaners
- a milk bottle lid or something similar
- two wooden spoons/teaspoons
- Blu Tack
- small plastic figures

Instructions

1. Trim the piece of white paper to the size of the aluminium tray and use a small amount of PVA glue to stick it inside the base.

2. If you like, use the red and blue crayons to draw some ice-hockey arena line markings on the piece of paper.

3. Fill two thirds of the tray with water and put it in the freezer overnight.

4. Twist a pipe cleaner into a square shape and bend the square in the middle to make a goal. Repeat this step to make two goals.

5. Once the water has frozen, challenge a friend to a game of ice hockey using a bottle cap as a puck and wooden spoons or teaspoons as hockey sticks. Position the goals at either end of the tray. On your marks, get set, play!

Your tabletop ice rink is also perfect for ice skating! Here's how you could make some mini ice skaters:

1 Use a small piece of Blu Tack to stick a few toy figures (such as a LEGO figurine) into the base of an ice-cube tray. This will hold the figures in place so that they won't topple over.

2 Fill the ice-cube tray with water and put it in the freezer.

3 Once the ice cubes have frozen, pop them out of the tray and use the ice blocks to skate the figurines over the ice!

4 Use the teaspoons to move the figurines around. Maybe you could choreograph an ice-skating routine?!

You could even pick up some pebbles and a toothbrush and have a go at Tabletop Curling!

IN CASE YOU'RE WONDERING WHAT CURLING IS, IT'S A WONDERFULLY WACKY SPORT WHERE PEOPLE TAKE IT IN TURNS TO AGGRESSIVELY SWEEP SOME ICE WITH A FUNNY-LOOKING BROOM TO HELP MAKE A GIANT ROCK GLIDE TOWARDS A TARGET, ALL WHILE BEING YELLED AT BY THEIR TEAMMATES. IT'S DEFINITELY ONE OF THE MORE CURIOUS WINTER ACTIVITIES!

WHO INVENTED WRAPPING PAPER?

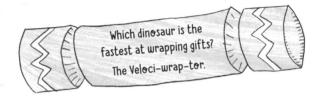

Which dinosaur is the fastest at wrapping gifts?
The Veloci-wrap-tor.

After all that action, we should head inside to warm up. We can make hot chocolate, pop on a cheesy Christmas film and wrap some presents. Wrapping Christmas presents for my friends and family is something I look forward to every year. It keeps the gifts a surprise and the little decorative details make each package feel extra special. Talking of surprises . . . Puddles, is that for me?

HELP!

CAN YOU GUESS WHAT IT IS?

Perhaps we should rescue Nigel from all that gift wrap and see if we can learn a little bit about the tradition of wrapping presents at the same time. After all, it looks like Puddles could do with some help!

THE FIRST WRAPPING PAPER

Before paper, humans carved pictures and symbols into stone and bone. Early humans were very skilled at it, but it was super time-consuming, so they needed something light that could be carried around to help them communicate more quickly.

Around 5,000 years ago, the ancient Egyptians came up with a solution and began to use ink on a tall, grass-like plant named **papyrus**. Nowadays papyrus is quite rare, but it used to grow along the river Nile, so it was very common in ancient Egypt. To turn it into a paper-like material, the stem of the papyrus plant was cut into thin strips that were then laid side by side in columns. A sticky resin from the plant was spread on top of the strips and acted like glue. Then a second layer of papyrus strips was placed in rows on top of the first layer. Finally, everything was pressed together and left to dry in the hot Egyptian sun.

Quality papyrus was saved for writing important documents and religious texts, but the scrappy, rough pieces of papyrus were used by merchants to wrap up their goods. So papyrus was one of the earliest forms of wrapping paper!

JAPANESE FUROSHIKI

Furoshiki is a square-shaped Japanese wrapping cloth that has been used in Japan since 170 CE (that's about 1,300 years ago!) At first, it was mostly used to wrap important objects and treasures found in temples, but it later became a popular way to wrap clothing.

When people visited a Japanese bathhouse, they would wrap their kimonos in fabric *furoshiki* cloths while they bathed in the warm waters. Often, the square pieces of fabric were decorated with family symbols, so that guests wouldn't confuse their kimonos with other people's. It didn't take long for the idea of *furoshiki* wrapping to spread and soon it was being used to wrap all sorts of things, including food, books and gifts.

KOREAN BOJAGI

The word *bojagi* roughly translates as 'wrapping' and is the general name given to patchwork Korean wrapping cloth. *Bojagi* is an important part of Korean culture and has long been used to wrap, carry and store precious objects for religious rituals and marriages. They can be made from one large piece of decorated fabric or stitched together from scraps in patterns known as *jogakbo*. Some of the oldest surviving examples are from the 1390s (about 640 years ago!), a time when Korean women were expected to stay at home and do household chores like mending clothes. *Bojagi* became a way for these women to express themselves, using leftover pieces of material to create beautiful, patterned designs.

EXTRAVAGANT VICTORIAN GIFT WRAP

Over in the UK, it wasn't until the Victorian period that gift wrapping became really popular. As printing technology improved in the nineteenth century, the tradition of sending Christmas cards became more common, and manufacturers started printing matching designs on tissue paper for wrapping gifts. The Victorians really went to town on the Christmas wrapping, with plenty of shiny metallic materials and velvet ribbon or lace. They sometimes used thick paper designed with a swirly pattern that looked a bit like a marble, in a technique called – *ahem* – **marbling**.

THE HALLMARK BROTHERS

The printed wrapping paper that we use today was actually invented by accident. In 1917, two brothers called Joyce and Rollie Hall were running a stationery shop in Kansas City, USA. The pair sold A LOT of tissue paper, which was the Christmas gift wrap of choice at the time, and one day they completely ran out. They quickly found a stack of thin patterned paper – meant for lining envelopes – and decided to rename it and sell it as 'gift wrap'. The paper was an immediate success, and soon the brothers were making and selling their own printed paper designed especially for wrapping gifts. The wrapping paper industry was born in this way, and the brothers named their company 'Hallmark'.

ECO-WRAPPING!

So it was the Hall brothers who developed the rolls of gift wrap that have become popular around the world. And when I say popular, I mean POPULAR. One estimate suggests that in the UK *alone* people throw away around 227,000 miles of wrapping paper over the Christmas period. That's enough to stretch all the way to the Moon! Sadly, not all gift wrap is recyclable and most of it is made from wood that comes from chopping down trees. Our trees provide homes for wildlife and help us combat climate change, so it's important to save on paper and protect our trees when we can. (Especially if we want to wrap BIG things, such as giant yetis.)

Here are some ideas for more sustainable ways to wrap Christmas presents that you could try at home!

- **If your family does decide to buy gift wrap, it's best to avoid paper with metallic foil and glitter as these definitely won't be recyclable.**

- **Another helpful way to check if your paper can be recycled is the 'scrunch test'. If it scrunches, and stays scrunched, it can probably be popped in the recycling bin and used to make something new.**

- Instead of fancy gift wrap, why not use plain brown paper that's *both* recyclable and compostable instead? You could also get creative and transform it into beautiful patterned paper using festive stamps and ink, or even try the Victorian marbling technique.

- Challenge yourself to unwrap your presents as carefully as possible so you can fold up the paper and reuse it again.

- Go on a nature hunt and look for pinecones, sprigs of herbs or evergreen plants to use to decorate your presents, rather than using foil bows or glitter.

- Just like Japanese *furoshiki* and Korean *bojagi*, you could swap wrapping paper for wrapping cloth. Wrapping cloth is more sustainable than paper because it can be used again and again. You could even ask a Big Elf to help you cut up your old clothes to make wrapping cloth.

- Rather than paper or fabric you could reuse baskets, jars and boxes to hold your presents.

- There's always the option to avoid wrapping presents altogether! Why not hide gifts around the house and make a scavenger hunt with clues to follow so you keep the element of surprise?!

UMMM . . . PUDDLES?!

HOW IS TINSEL MADE?

Perhaps one of the most popular things we decorate with at Christmas is tinsel! To be honest, I'm surprised we've made it all the way to page 208 without mentioning the sparkly stuff. We hang these glittering garlands just about anywhere, from Christmas trees to staircase banisters, fireplaces, desks, doorways, bunk beds, picture frames, cupboard doors . . . in fact there are very few things you can't Christmas-ify with a touch of tinsel.

In the UK, we LOVE tinsel, with around 12 MILLION metres being made here every year. That's enough tinsel to stretch all the way from the Christmas tree in London's Trafalgar Square to the one at the famous Rockefeller Center in New York City. You could say that we have a serious case of tinsel-litus . . .

?

DID YOU KNOW . . .

The word tinsel comes from an Old French word *estincele*, which means sparkle.

Today, these tremendous amounts of tinsel are made from a material called polyvinyl chloride, or PVC for short. It's a type of thin, flexible plastic that is given a special treatment to make it look glossy and metallic. But tinsel was originally a small, heavy, hanging decoration made from actual silver! A metalworker would heat and hammer the precious metal into shiny strands that could be hung on branches. But it was extremely expensive, so not everyone could afford it. Over time, the material changed to the cheaper PVC and the handcrafted method has been replaced with factory machines that can make a LOT of tinsel really quickly.

A modern tinsel garland machine looks a bit like a candy floss maker – but how does it work?

- **Tinsel starts as a LONG strip of shiny PVC wound round a reel like a ribbon. The first step is to choose the colour you want your tinsel to be!**

- **The reel of PVC is loaded on to the tinsel garland machine. The loose end of the material is carefully fed into the top part of the machine, and the reel hangs on a rod so it can spin and unwind the material as it is pulled through.**

- **First, the PVC passes through a set of cutters. These shred the edges of the metallic plastic into little fringes.**

- **Next, the shredded PVC is pulled through a set of rollers and a thin wire is laid down the centre of the material. (This is what will hold the tinsel together.)**

- **The PVC and the wire are fed into a rotating drum, which spins and twists the two materials around each other. This part looks just like a candy floss maker, which spins hot strands of sugar into cloud-like candy.**

- **We're almost done. When the PVC comes out of the drum it has been transformed into fluffy tinsel! All that's left to do is cut it into lengths and send it off to the shops for people to buy and decorate with at Christmas.**

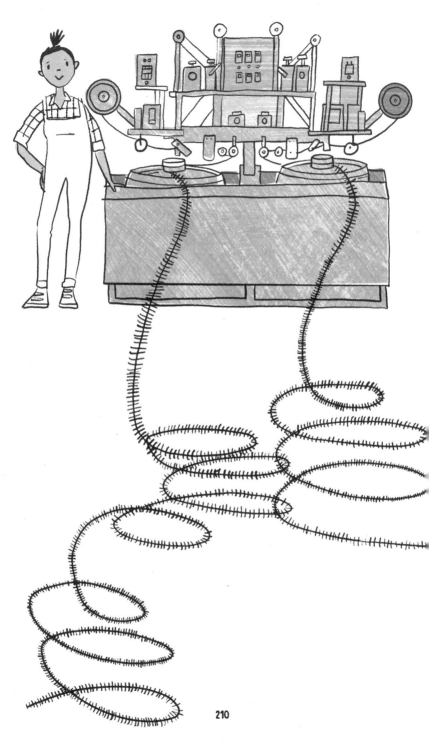

Tinsel is a fun, sparkly decoration but it's useful to know that it's rarely recyclable. It's important to store it carefully so it doesn't get squashed or tangled, as that way we can use it again and again, year after year. But if tinsel doesn't leave you feeling dazzled, then there are lots of other Christmas decoration ideas you can try – including the handmade ones in this book!

? DID YOU KNOW . . .
Tinsel was originally designed to reflect the warm glow of candles hanging on the Christmas tree.

I don't know about you, but to me the thought of having ACTUAL burning candles on a tree seems kind of dangerous! Come to think of it, this brings us nicely to our next question . . .

HOW DO CANDLES WORK?

Thankfully, we don't put real candles on our Christmas trees any more – we've swapped the potential fire hazard for much safer fairy lights! But candles are still a big part of Christmas and are sometimes used to represent the Star of Bethlehem, which guided the Three Kings to the stable where Baby Jesus was born. Personally, I like to use scented candles because they fill my home with delicious Christmassy smells like pine trees, cinnamon and peppermint. But how do candles work?

What happened when the elves used up Father Christmas's favourite candle?

He was INCENSED.

Candles have two main parts: a **wick** and **wax**.

A **wick** is usually made from thin strands of cotton that have been twisted or braided together. But they can also be made with small strips of wood, or tightly rolled paper.

Candle **wax** can be made from lots of different things too, but these days most candle wax is made from something called **paraffin**. Paraffin comes from **petroleum**, or 'petrol', which is a type of fossil fuel that we sometimes use as fuel for our cars. But today, wax is also made with fats that come from plants and animals. For example, soy wax is made from the oils that come from soybeans; tallow is the name we give to the fat that comes from cooking animal meat; and beeswax is made in hives by honeybees!

BUSY BEES

When a female honeybee is between twelve and twenty days old, she develops four pairs of **glands** on the bottom of her **abdomen** (or tummy). A gland is a special organ that produces something, like sweat, tears or in this case, beeswax! Liquid wax oozes out of the honeybee's glands and hardens into tiny flakes when it comes into contact with the air. Next, the bee will use stiff hairs on her back legs to scrape the wax from her abdomen and passes it forward to her mouth. She'll use her **mandibles** (or mouthparts) to chew the wax until it's soft, then she will carefully spit it out and shape it into the hexagonal cells that make honeycomb inside a hive!

Beeswax was one of the first materials used to make candles, but throughout history, they've been made from some very bizarre things indeed . . . Turn the page to find out more!

A POTTED HISTORY OF CURIOUS CANDLES

3,000 BCE (about 5,000 years ago)

Long before candles with wicks, the ancient Egyptians simply dipped reeds into melted animal fat and lit them to use as torches.

500 BCE (about 2,500 years ago)

The ancient Romans are thought to have created the first wicked candles. They would take a roll of papyrus paper and dip it into melted animal fat or beeswax till the wax layers built up and looked something like the candles we use today.

200 BCE (about 2,200 years ago)

In China, rolled rice paper was burned in a wax made with fats and oils that came from crushed insects and seeds.

1 CE
(about 2,100 years ago)

Indigenous communities in North America used small fish as their candles. Eulachon, or 'candlefish',

are so oily that they could be dried, placed on a forked stick and burned as a candle without the need for any wick at all. (I think Puddles would love a birthday cake decorated with candlefish!)

1800s/1900s
(about 200 years ago)

In the nineteenth and twentieth centuries, hunting whales had become a big business. People used whale meat and blubber for food and fuel, but sperm whales were also hunted for a special substance called spermaceti. Spermaceti is a rich, waxy oil produced by an organ in sperm whales' heads and was used to make candles. Thankfully, a ban to stop people from whaling for money-making reasons was introduced in 1986. Although it hasn't protected whales completely, it does mean we don't use these majestic animals for making candles any more.

We certainly won't be dipping reeds in fat or setting fire to any fish today, but we do want to find out how candles burn and stay alight.

HOW DOES A CANDLE WORK?

When you light the wick with a flame from a match or lighter, the heat from the flame quickly travels downwards to the wax beneath. It doesn't take much heat to melt the wax, so it almost instantly turns into a liquid. This is why there is always a little pool of melted wax around the base of the wick.

This liquid wax is drawn up through the wick (a bit like a chimney). But as it travels up the wick, the liquid gets hotter and evaporates. This means it turns into a gas.

The wax gas reacts with **oxygen** in the air to create heat, light, water vapour and a gas called **carbon dioxide**. This chemical reaction is called **combustion**.

The carbon dioxide around the flame then starts to burn, acting as fuel for the fire. The candle flame stays lit because of the burning wax gas, not the burning wick.

Heat from the flame travels in different directions, which helps keep the candle burning. We call this movement of heat **conduction** and **convection**. Conduction is when heat from the flame travels down the wick and continues to melt more wax at the top of the candle. Convection pulls the hot gas away from the wick and sucks oxygen from the surrounding air into the base of the flame. This provides the flame with a constant supply of oxygen, which keep the wax gas burning!

HOW TO RELIGHT A CANDLE – WITHOUT TOUCHING IT!

You will need

- a candle
- matches

Instructions

1 Ask a Big Elf to light a candle and let it burn for about 30 seconds.

2 Get your Big Elf ready to light another match.

3 Blow out the candle flame with a quick puff of breath as your Big Elf lights the match.

4 Place the flame of the match into the wisps of smoke that you should see rising from the wick and watch closely.

5 You should see the flame jump from the match to the candle wick without having to touch it all!

THE SCIENCE BIT

This happens because even after you blow out the candle, the wick stays hot for a while, so the wax continues to melt and evaporate into a gas. The wax gas is drawn up and out of the wick, so when your Big Elf brings the lit match close to the wick (without touching it!), the gas catches fire and relights the candle. You have just proved that a candle flame comes from the burning gas, not the wick!

Right, so now you know the science behind those twinkly Christmas candles, but can you think of any other festivals that involve candles?

OOH IT'S DEFINITLY MY BIRTHDAY THIS TIME!

Sigh. No, Puddles it's still not your birthday . . . It's DIWALI!

CURIOUS QUESTIONS ABOUT . . . DIWALI!

Diwali is the five-day Festival of Lights celebrated by millions of Hindus, Sikhs and Jains across the world. It's a festival of new beginnings, the triumph of good over evil and light over darkness. The date Diwali starts changes each year because it follows the pattern of the Moon in the Hindu calendar, but it usually happens between mid-October and mid-November.

WHAT IS THE STORY OF DIWALI?

Here to tell us a bit more about why and how they celebrate Diwali are eight-year-old Karina and her mummy Bhanu, who live in northwest London with her daddy and little brother, Aran.

KARINA

BHANU

HI, KARINA! I HEAR YOU LOVE DIWALI AND ARE THE PERFECT PERSON TO CHAT TO. I WONDER, IS THERE A STORY BEHIND THE FESTIVAL?

YES! IN THE STORY, A DEMON CALLED RAVANA TAKES SITA AND LOCKS HER AWAY, SO THE GREAT PRINCE RAMA AND THE MONKEY KING, HANUMAN, SAVE SITA AND KILL RAVANA.

Diwali is celebrated throughout India and around the world, so there are many different stories surrounding the festival. Karina and her family are Hindu, and they tell the story of Rama and Sita and their triumph over evil . . .

Long ago, there was a great prince called Rama, who had a beautiful wife called Sita.

A terrible demon king called Ravana – who had ten heads and twenty arms – heard of Sita's beauty and planned to kidnap her. He used a magical golden deer to distract the prince, and once Sita was alone, the demon king kidnapped her and flew her away on his chariot. Rama set out to rescue Sita, and on his search he met the monkey king, Hanuman, who agreed to help. Hanuman sent messages to all the monkeys in the land to go and look for Sita.

Hanuman and the monkeys found Sita imprisoned on the island of Lanka, and they fought a mighty battle that lasted ten days. It looked as though Ravana was going to win the fight, until Rama used his special bow and arrow that had the power of the gods. Rama shot Ravana with the arrow and the battle was won!

Rama and Sita were reunited, and they began their long journey home. As it got dark, the people of the kingdom put out little oil lamps to guide them safely back.

WHAT ARE DIVAS?

Just like the lamps that guided Rama and Sita on their way home, Karina's family light lamps called *divas* at Diwali as a reminder that light triumphs over dark and good triumphs over evil. Traditionally, *divas* (or *diyas*) are made from clay. They are formed by pressing your thumb into a ball of clay and shaping it into a shallow pot. Then they are baked in a kiln –which is like a REALLY hot oven – until they harden and can be painted in bright colours. *Divas* can be filled with oil, candles or little electric tealights to bring light to people's homes.

But *divas* aren't the only thing people use to decorate with at Diwali . . .

WHAT ARE RANGOLI?

RANGOLI ARE PICTURES WE PAINT ON THE FLOOR ABOUT DIWALI. I MAKE THEM OUT OF PAINT WITH LOTS OF DOTS AND COOL SHAPES LIKE HEARTS.

During Diwali, *rangoli* patterns are made on the floor by the front of the house to welcome guests and bring good luck. These special patterns can be made with brightly coloured rice, paint, powder, sand and even leaves and petals! They are usually symmetrical and include images of hearts, flowers and other things from nature.

WHAT SPECIAL FOODS ARE EATEN DURING DIWALI?

ONE OF MY FAVOURITE THINGS ABOUT HOLIDAYS IS THE FOOD. WHAT DO YOU EAT AT DIWALI?

WELL, WE HAVE SOME CURRIES, INDIAN SWEETS, INDIAN SNACKS, DAHL AND CAKE! I LIKE DAHL THE MOST. IT'S MADE OUT OF LENTILS.

WE PREPARE A LOT OF INDIAN SNACKS AND SWEETS IN ADVANCE BECAUSE IT TAKES A LONG TIME TO MAKE THEM. THAT COULD INCLUDE SNACKS LIKE *PAKORAS* AND *SAMOSAS*, AND SWEETS SUCH AS *GULAB JAMUN* AND *LADOO*.

Pakoras are crispy fritters made from vegetables and potatoes that have been deep-fried in flour or batter.

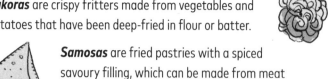

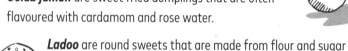

Samosas are fried pastries with a spiced savoury filling, which can be made from meat or potatoes, peas and onions.

Gulab jamun are sweet fried dumplings that are often flavoured with cardamom and rose water.

Ladoo are round sweets that are made from flour and sugar that has been fried in small pieces and then shaped into balls.

WE GIVE THE SWEETS AND SNACKS TO FRIENDS AND FAMILY AS GIFTS AND OFFER THEM TO WHOEVER COMES TO OUR HOUSE ON DIWALI. MY MUM (KARINA'S GRANDMA) MAKES THEM FOR THE WHOLE FAMILY!

THAT'S BRILLIANT, KARINA, DO YOU THINK YOUR GRANDMA WILL GIVE US A RECIPE FOR SOME OF HER SPECIAL INDIAN SWEETS?

YEAH!

I THINK SHE'D LOVE THAT!

KARINA'S NANI'S
COCONUT LADOO

You will need

- 400g desiccated coconut
- 1 x 400g can of condensed milk
- a spoon
- a tray

For decorating

- desiccated coconut
- milk chocolate
- white chocolate
- two microwaveable bowls
- hundreds-and-thousands sprinkles

Instructions

1 Put the desiccated coconut and condensed milk into a mixing bowl.

2 Using a spoon, stir the two ingredients together till all the coconut is covered in the condensed milk.

3 Roll the coconut mixture into tablespoon-size balls, place on to a tray and refrigerate.

These are your simple coconut *ladoos*!

To decorate with coconut: Roll the *ladoos* in dry desiccated coconut till they are coated.

To decorate with chocolate: Break the milk and white chocolate into pieces and place them in separate microwavable bowls. Ask your Big Elf to help you melt the chocolate however you like to do it in your family – I like to use the microwave! – and gently heat it until it is entirely liquid.

Dip the *ladoos* into the melted chocolate and sprinkle with desiccated coconut, hundreds-and-thousands or drizzle with the other kind of chocolate before it sets.

Keep your *ladoos* refrigerated in an airtight container.

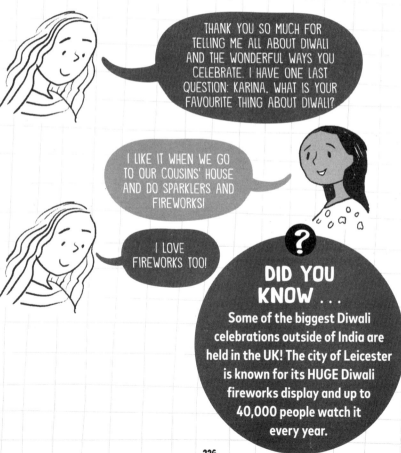

THANK YOU SO MUCH FOR TELLING ME ALL ABOUT DIWALI AND THE WONDERFUL WAYS YOU CELEBRATE. I HAVE ONE LAST QUESTION: KARINA. WHAT IS YOUR FAVOURITE THING ABOUT DIWALI?

I LIKE IT WHEN WE GO TO OUR COUSINS' HOUSE AND DO SPARKLERS AND FIREWORKS!

I LOVE FIREWORKS TOO!

DID YOU KNOW . . .
Some of the biggest Diwali celebrations outside of India are held in the UK! The city of Leicester is known for its HUGE Diwali fireworks display and up to 40,000 people watch it every year.

FIREWORKS IN A JAR

Fireworks are loud, exciting explosions of colour that are used not only for Diwali but for celebrations all around the world. They may look epic, but they can also be dangerous, so most firework displays use trained professionals called **firework technicians**, who wear special safety gear (doesn't that sound like a seriously cool job?!).

The good news is that this activity means you can make your own mini fireworks displays safely at home all year round!

You will need

- a jam jar or similar clear container
- two tablespoons of cooking oil (any oil will do!)
- a small bowl or dish
- food colouring (as many colours as you like)
- a fork

Instructions

Make sure you ask permission from your Big Elf before you have fun with this colourful activity.

1. Fill the jar with warm water, leaving a little space at the top.
2. Measure two tablespoons of oil into the small dish.
3. Add a few drops of food colouring to the oil and give it a stir with a fork.
4. Dump the oil with the food colouring into the jar of water and get ready to watch the 'fireworks'!

At first, the oil and food colouring will float to the top and separate from the water. Next, you'll see the food colouring start to separate from the oil and sink down into the water. As the food colouring mixes with the water it will appear to burst, just like fireworks in the sky!

THE SCIENCE BIT – WHAT MAKES THE COLOURS SEPARATE?

You may have heard that 'oil and water don't mix'. This is true! But why?

Well, oil and water molecules REALLY don't like each other. In fact, they dislike each other so much that if you put oil and water together in a jar and leave them alone, they start pushing and trying to get as far away from each other as possible. Rude!

Food colouring is 'water soluble', which means it likes water, so if it had to choose between the two, food colouring is much happier with water than it would be with oil.

When you pour the food colouring into the oil and stir it with a fork, the two will mix and hang out for a short time. However, when you pour them both into the water, the oil molecules will eventually shove the water out of the way and take themselves to the top of the jar. Meanwhile, the food colouring finds its way out of the oil and heads into the water, which it prefers!

This experiment also shows us that liquids can have different densities. You might remember from Sinking Satsumas (pages 33–34) that everything in the world is made of tiny bits that we can't see called atoms. The density of an object depends on how heavy its atoms are and how closely those atoms are packed together. We also learned that something will float on water if it is the same or less dense than water. In this experiment, we see that the oil is less dense than the water, so the oil floats. But the food colouring is more dense than the oil, so it sinks down through the oil into the water, where it gets mixed up!

MADDIE'S CURIOUS CHRISTMAS QUIZ – ROUND FOUR

It's time for ROUND FOUR of my mega quiz. Get your pen and papyrus at the ready . . .

1. What is the name of the explosive chemical that makes crackers go BANG?

2. A nutcracker is an example of what type of simple machine?

3. What are two different ways that fairy lights can be wired into a circuit?

4. What is the name of the funny male actor who dresses up as a woman in pantomime?

5. What is the name of the simple machine that can help stage technicians pull an actor up in the air and make them fly?

6. How does Puddles the penguin get down hills in Antarctica?

7. What force might slow down a toboggan?

8. What is the name for Japanese wrapping cloth?

9. What material was tinsel first made out of?

10. What animal was once used as a candle in North America?

Answers on page 233

SNOW LONG, FAREWELL!

As the firework display comes to an end and the night sky returns to darkness, it's time for us to wrap up our curious Christmas journey and think back to all the amazing things we've learned.

We explored the origins of our festive traditions and discovered some new ones along the way. Who'd have thought that Father Christmas occasionally wears a Hawaiian shirt, or that presents can also be delivered by a festive goat, a bunch of naughty trolls or a charming witch on a broomstick?

We embraced the frosty weather and revealed the secrets of our natural world in winter. We even spotted some unexpected Christmas animals – I won't be forgetting the gruesome sea angel or the epic journey of the Christmas Island red crabs any time soon!

We tucked into the history of holiday food and had tons of fun zooming down slopes, soaring through theatres and decorating the house with magical lights. Hopefully you've even tried making your own decorations or attempted one of our cool Christmas activities at home.

From me, Puddles and Nigel, thank you so much for reading this book. We hope it's left you feeling full of festive spirit and bursting with curiosity!

All that's left for us to say is . . .

We wish you a very Merry Christmas and a Happy New Year!

Seasons Greetings!

Happy Solstice!

Shubh Diwali!

Hanukkah Sameach!

Xīnnián kuàilè / 新年快樂!

Happy Holidays!

HAPPY BIRTHDAY!

MERRY SNOWMAS!

(Not quite, you two . . .)

P.S. If you're STILL reading this book while tucked up in bed on Christmas Eve, then you REALLY have to go to sleep now. Go on. Put the book down. It's a big day tomorrow!

Night night, sleep tight, so Father Christmas can stay out of sight.

ANSWERS

Round One

1. The Nativity
2. Flamingo
3. 364
4. Coca-Cola
5. 'The Night Before Christmas'
6. Saint Nicholas, the fourth-century Greek bishop from Myra
7. Thirteen
8. Gold, frankincense and myrrh
9. Norway
10. Cucumber (or a pickle!)

Round Two

1. Click! (The click is made by a special tendon in one of their feet.)
2. Ice
3. Roald Amundsen
4. Blubber
5. Sea snail
6. A speck of dust
7. Another planet!
8. Summer
9. Hedgehog
10. Closed

Round Three

1. Pickled boar's head
2. The Americas (what is now Mexico)
3. KFC
4. The bath
5. Sulphur
6. Bogs
7. From the minced meat they used to be filled with
8. An unopened flower bud
9. *Hansel and Gretel*
10. Pulling

Round Four

1. Silver fulminate
2. Lever
3. Series and parallel
4. The dame
5. Pulley
6. Tobogganing
7. Friction
8. *Furoshiki*
9. Silver
10. Candlefish (eulachon)

Did you find all the gingerbread men? They were on the following pages: 13, 16, 18, 33, 41, 45, 56, 61, 64, 69, 79, 92, 97, 104, 118, 127, 162, 170, 192, 196, 201, 211, 214, 230, 233

SOURCES

I consulted lots of different sources while researching this book – here is a selection in case you want to find out more about the science and history of Christmas!

What Is Christmas? www.whychristmas.com; *Lights, Camel, Action! It's Strictly the Nativity* by Antony Copus, © 2016 Out of the Ark Ltd. 'What is Christmas?', www.bbc.co.uk/bitesize **Why Is Christmas on 25 December?** 'Why is Christmas in December?', www.britannica.com; 'Why is Christmas on Dec. 25?', Valeria Strauss, www.washingtonpost.com
What Are the Twelve Days of Christmas? 'The Tudors: The Twelve Days of Christmas', www.english-heritage.org.uk; 'The Maths of the Twelve Days of Christmas', Tom Crawford, www.seh.ox.ac.uk
Who Is Father Christmas? / Why Does Father Christmas Wear Red? 'Christmas: The History of Father Christmas', Tom Moriarty, www.english-heritage.org.uk; 'Santa Claus', www.britannica.com; 'The origin and evolution of Father Christmas', www.york.ac.uk; 'The real reason Father Christmas wears red and white', www.bbc.co.uk
Why Do We Get Presents in Stockings? 'The Legend of the Christmas Stocking', Emily Spivack, www.smithsonianmag.com
How Do Christmas Presents Get Delivered? 'The Icelandic Yule Lads and Gryla: Iceland's Christmas Trolls', Richard Chapman, www.guidetoiceland.is; 'Three Kings Day', www.kids.nationalgeographic.com; 'Epiphany: What is Epiphany and How is it Celebrated?', www.bbc.co.uk/newsround; 'The Befana', www.italyheritage.com
Why Do We Have Christmas Trees? 'How to tell the difference between Douglas Fir, Spruce and Pine Trees', www.totallywilduk.co.uk; 'Why do we have Christmas trees? The surprising history behind this holiday tradition', www.nationalgeographic.com; 'The Ukrainian Tradition of Spiderwebs and Christmas',

www.ukraine.com; 'The Mysterious Tradition of Hiding a Pickle on Christmas Trees', Paula Meija, www.atlastobscura.com
Curious Questions About . . . Hanukkah! 'Discover the History of Latkes During Hanukkah', Tori Avey, www.pbs.org; 'Hanukkah: What is the Jewish festival all about?', www.bbc.co.uk; 'Hanukkah', www.kids.nationalgeographic.com
How Do Reindeer Fly? 'Caribou', www.kids.nationalgeographic.com; '4 Facts to Know About Reindeer', *SciShow Kids*, www.youtube.com
Where Is the North Pole? / Who Discovered the North Pole? 'North Pole', www.education.nationalgeographic.org
How Do Animals Stay Warm in the Arctic? 'How Animals Stay Warm with Blubber', www.scientificamerican.com
How Are Snowflakes Made? 'Where Do Snowflakes Come From?', *SciShow Kids*, www.youtube.com
Why Are the Days So Short at Christmas Time? 'What's the winter solstice?', www.kids.nationalgeographic.com; 'What causes Earth's seasons?', www.spaceplace.nasa.gov
What Is Winter Solstice? 'Yule', www.britannica.com; 'Festival of Zayeshmehr (Yalda)', Massoume Price, www.cais-soas.com; 'Yuzu Bath — A Japanese Tradition for the Winter Solstice', www.jcccw.org
Why Is Holly Spiky? 'Hollies Get Prickly for a Reason', www.nationalgeographic.com
Why Do People Kiss Under the Mistletoe? 'Why do people kiss under the mistletoe?', www.bbc.co.uk/newsround
What's Inside a Pinecone? 'Unlocking the Secrets of the Pinecone', Megan Arnett, www.scientificamerican.com
The Curious Christmas Creature Gallery! 'What Are Christmas Tree Worms?', www.oceanservice.noaa.gov; 'Starry Night Cracker Butterfly', www.reimangardens.com; 'Sea angel', www.montereybayaquarium.org; 'Tinkerbella

nana, a new species of fairyfly',
www.phys.org; 'Candy Cane Shrimp',
www. ocean.si.edu; 'Christmas Island Red Crab',
www.kids.nationalgeographic.com

Why Do We Have Turkey at Christmas?
'How the turkey conquered Christmas',
www.bbc.com; 'Christmas: Christmas Dinners
Through History', www.english-heritage.org.uk

**What Do People Around the World Eat for
Christmas Dinner?** 'Why Japan Celebrates
Christmas with KFC', Eric Barton, www.bbc.com;
'Christmas Dinner in 25 Countries Around the
World', Bianca Bahamondes, www.insider.com;
'In Slovakia, Christmas Dinner Starts in
The Bathtub', Meghan Collins Sullivan,
www.npr.org; 'The Painted Murals of San
Bartolo', www.whc.unesco.org

**How Do Astronauts Eat Christmas Dinner
in Space?** 'Celebrating the Holiday Season in
Space', www.nasa.gov; 'Christmas Dinner on the
International Space Station', Amanda Fiegl,
www.smithsonianmag.com

Why Do Brussels Sprouts Make You Fart?
'Why Do Brussels Sprouts Make You Fart?',
Sarah Castor-Perry,
www.thenakedscientists.com

How Do Cranberries Grow? 'About the Harvest',
www.oceanspray.com

Why Do We Build Gingerbread Houses?
'Meat to Sweat: A History of the Mince Pie',
Sam Bilton, www.english-heritage.org.uk;
'No Innocent Spice: The Secret Story of Nutmeg,
Life and Death', Allison Aubrey, www.npr.org

Where Do Gingerbread Houses Come From?
'A Short History of Gingerbread', Sam Bilton,
www.english-heritage.org

How Are Candy Canes Made? 'How Did
Candy Canes Get Their Shape?',
www.wonderopolis.org

**Curious Questions About . . . Chinese New
Year!** 'Chinese and Lunar New Year',
www.bbc.co.uk/cbeebies; 'Which Lunar New
Year Animal Are You?', Elizabeth Hilfrank,
www.kids.nationalgeographic.com;

Why Do Crackers Go Bang? 'Why Do Christmas
Crackers Go Bang?', www.sciencefocus.com;
www.tomsmith-crackers.com

How Do Nutcrackers Work?
www.nutcrackermuseum.com; 'Levers',
www.dkfindout.com

How Do Fairy Lights Work? 'How do fairy lights
work?' www.youtube.com

What Is Pantomime? 'The Story of Pantomime',
www.vam.ac.uk; 'It's behind you! A look into the
history of pantomime', www.york.ac.uk

How Do Pantomime Fairies Fly? 'Flying into
Physics: Pulleys and Pulley Systems',
www.vimeo.com

How Do You Make a Toboggan Go Faster?
'How to Make a Sled Go Faster, According to
Science', Lucas Reilly, www.mentalfloss.com;
'The Fastest Sled Ride Ever!', *SciShow Kids*,
www.youtube.com

Who Invented Wrapping Paper? 'Wrappers'
Delight: A Brief History of Wrapping Paper',
Megan Garber, www.atlantic.com

How Is Tinsel Made? 'Where Does Tinsel Come
From?', www.bbc.co.uk/newsround

How Do Candles Work? www.candles.org;
'Candle chemistry', www.rigb.org

Curious Questions About . . . Diwali! 'Diwali:
What is it?', www.bbc.co.uk; 'What is a Rangoli
Pattern?', www.twinkl.co.uk

Gingerbread Template
If you fancy having a go at some gingerneering,
here are links to useful templates you can use!
https://media.immediate.co.uk/volatile/
sites/30/2011/12/gingerbread-1-7fdf03a.pdf
https://media.immediate.co.uk/volatile/
sites/30/2011/12/gretels-grotto-1-8d3055b.pdf

A CURIOUS COMPENDIUM OF WORDS

Here are some definitions of the cool science words and phrases we covered in this book, in case you're feeling curious about what they mean!

Acids and **alkalis**: In chemistry, almost all liquids (and substances that can be mixed with water) can be placed on a pH scale. This is a way of measuring how acidic or alkaline a liquid is using numbers 0–14. Acids have a pH of less than 7 and include things such as lemon juice. Alkalis have a pH of more than 7 and include things such as soapy water. Liquids with a pH of 7 are called neutral. An alkali can be brought down to pH 7, or neutralized, by adding acid. Some strong acids and alkalis can be dangerous, so we should always be careful when handling certain substances.

Adaptation: When a plant or animal's body or behaviour changes over time to help it survive in its environment.

Atoms: The tiniest particles that make up everything in the universe, including air, water and even planets. Groups of atoms bonded together are called 'molecules'. We generally call atoms and molecules 'particles'.

Buoyancy: The upward force of water pushing on an object sitting in water. If the weight of the object is greater than the buoyancy, the object will sink. If the buoyancy is greater than the weight of the object, it will float.

Circuit: A complete path that allows electricity to flow around it. It's often made up of wires and electrical parts like batteries and light bulbs. Christmas tree lights are in either series or parallel circuits.

Combustion: The process of burning something, where a material reacts with oxygen to produce heat and light.

Condensation: When water in the form of gas cools down and turns into tiny liquid water droplets.

Conduction: The spreading of heat or electricity through a solid object. When atoms and molecules get hot they start to jiggle around and knock into cooler particles, passing on their heat energy.

Convection: When air or liquid warms up it rises. This makes cooler air or liquid take its place. This movement of heat is called convection.

Crystallization: The process in which a solid is formed as its atoms or molecules become organized in a rigid structure known as a crystal.

Defence mechanism: Ways in which animals or plants protect themselves from danger, such as hiding, running away, or using special features like camouflage.

Density: Measures how tightly packed particles are within a given amount of space.

Dissolve: When a solid substance mixes with a liquid and breaks down into much smaller bits to form a solution, such as sugar dissolving in water.

Enzymes: A special type of molecule found in our bodies and nature that helps with chemical reactions and digestion.

Evaporation: When a liquid changes into a gas, usually when it is heated – such as water turning into water vapour when it boils.

Friction: The force that happens when two objects rub against each other, often making it harder for them to slide over each other.

Fulcrum: The point on which a lever balances.

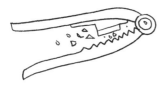

Hydrophilic: A hydrophilic molecule or substance is attracted to and bonds well with water.

Hydrophobic: A hydrophobic molecule or substance repels and does not bond well with water.

Lever: A simple machine that helps lift or move objects when a force is applied at one end, such as a seesaw.

Momentum: The amount of power an object has when it is moving, affecting how much force it can have on another object.

Mutualistic relationship: When two different species benefit from their interaction with each other.

Oesophagus: The muscular tube in our body that carries food from the mouth to the stomach.

Parallel circuit: A type of electrical circuit where electricity has multiple paths to flow through.

Pollination: The process of transferring pollen from the male part of a flower to the female part, which helps plants reproduce.

Pulley: A simple machine consisting of a wheel with a groove and a rope or chain around it, used to lift or lower objects.

Series circuit: A type of electrical circuit where electricity has a single path to flow through.

Small intestine: A long, tube-like organ that is part of the digestive system. Partly digested food passes from the stomach into the small intestine where lots of the nutrients from food are absorbed into the body.

Surface tension: When the surface of a liquid behaves like a stretchy elastic sheet. This is because liquid molecules pull together more tightly at the surface when they are in contact with air.

Water vapour: Water in the form of a gas.

PUFFIN BOOKS

UK | USA | Canada | Ireland | Australia
India | New Zealand | South Africa

Puffin is part of the Penguin Random House group of companies
whose addresses can be found at global.penguinrandomhouse.com.

www.penguin.co.uk www.puffin.co.uk www.ladybird.co.uk

First published 2023

001

Set in Mark Pro Condensed
Text design by Janene Spencer
Printed in Great Britain by Clays Ltd, Elcograf S.p.A.

The authorized representative in the EEA is Penguin Random House Ireland,
Morrison Chambers, 32 Nassau Street, Dublin D02 YH68

A CIP catalogue record for this book is available from the British Library

ISBN: 978-0-241-65254-1

All correspondence to:
Puffin Books
Penguin Random House Children's, One Embassy Gardens
8 Viaduct Gardens, London SW11 7BW

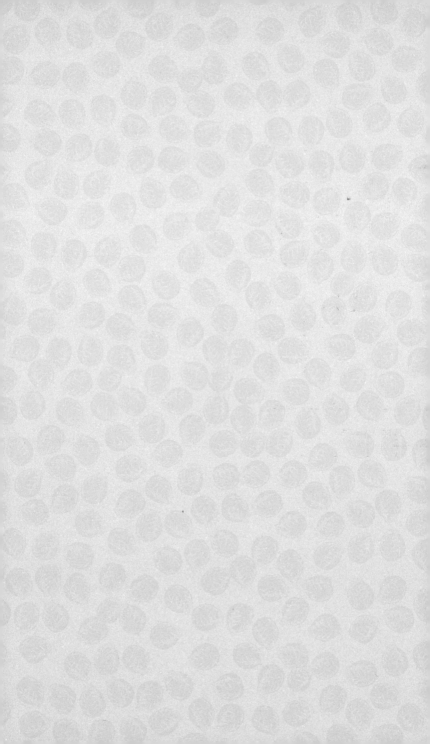